Warrior School

The Manual

Debbie Brewer

Written Words Publishing LLC
P.O. Box 462622
Aurora, Colorado 80046
www.writtenwordspublishing.com

Warrior School: The Manual © 2024 by Debbie Brewer.

All rights reserved. No part of this publication may be reproduced, stored in a retrieval system, or transmitted in any form by any means, electronic, mechanical, photocopying, recording, or otherwise, without the prior permission of the author.

Published by Written Words Publishing LLC December 1, 2024

ISBN: 978-1-961610-22-4 (paperback)
ISBN: 978-1-961610-23-1 (eBook)

Library of Congress Control Number: 2024924341

Cover designed by Written Words Publishing LLC

Manufactured and printed in the United States of America

All Scripture quotations, unless otherwise indicated, are taken from the New King James Version. Copyright © 1979, 1980, 1982 by Thomas Nelson, Inc. Used by permission. Scripture quotations noted as KJV are taken from the King James Version of the Bible, public domain. Scripture quotations noted as TPT are from The Passion Translation®. Copyright © 2017, 2018, 2020 by Passion & Fire Ministries, Inc. Used by permission. All rights reserved. ThePassionTranslation.com. Scripture quotations noted as AMP are taken from the Amplified® Bible (AMP), Copyright © 2015 by The Lockman Foundation. Used by permission of The Lockman Foundation. All rights reserved worldwide.

Table of Contents

Acknowledgments v
Introduction 1
Section I: Identity 3
    Chapter One: Relationship 5
    Chapter Two: Identity Crisis 9
    Chapter Three: Salvation 19
    Chapter Four: Identity Markers 39
Section II: Belief 55
    Chapter Five: What Do We Believe? 57
    Chapter Six: Faith 67
Section III: Purpose 85
    Chapter Seven: What Is Our Purpose? 87
    Chapter Eight: Dominion 97
Section IV: Liberation 123
    Chapter Nine: Liberated Liberators 125
    Chapter Ten: Lazarus 133
    Chapter Eleven: Setting People Free 145
Section V: Manifesting Christians 155
    Chapter Twelve: From Old to New 157
    Chapter Thirteen: Holy Spirit 161
    Chapter Fourteen: Manifestation 171
    Chapter Fifteen: Spiritual Hunger 177
    Chapter Sixteen: Take It 185

Section VI: To Catch a Thief 193
    Chapter Seventeen: The Thief Must Repay 195
    Chapter Eighteen: Prosperity 201
    Chapter Nineteen: Catching the Thief 211
Section VII: Weapons of Warfare 223
    Chapter Twenty: Kingdom 225
    Chapter Twenty-One: Armor of God 229
About the Author 249

Acknowledgments

I would like to thank all those who have attended Warrior Schools.

I would especially like to thank the first two warriors—Roxann and Traci. We were all brave to embark on this Holy Spirit led journey—and it continues.

Warriors, thank you for joining me in this preparation. It is God's intent that you be victorious and strong—not only for yourself, but for others. It is His desire to see His kingdom cover the earth!

> *"For the earth will be filled With the knowledge of the glory of the* LORD, *As the waters cover the sea"* (Habakkuk 2:14).

How much do the waters cover the sea? 100%! He wants the earth to be filled with heaven!!

I trust you walk away from this study:

- Knowing who you are in God
- Knowing your purpose
- Knowing what you believe
- Being liberated
- Manifesting the power of the Holy Spirit
- Seeing restoration
- Using your weapons for victory

Most of all, I hope it will stir your hunger for God!

I believe God will continue to speak to you and guide you wherever He takes you!

Warriors, arise!

Introduction

In late 2020, the Lord told me He was going to send me a couple. A couple of what, I wondered. I was not leading any group. I had not asked for a "couple," so I didn't know what He was talking about. A couple, as a man and woman? A couple of women? A couple of men?

I was riding to work one day, just talking with the Lord as I normally did. He said, "I want you to teach Warrior School." I answered, "Ok, but what is Warrior School?" He then began to talk to me about it. He started giving me chapters and subjects to cover. Then two women came to mind—a woman I was in a mentoring group with, along with my next door neighbor. There was the "couple."

Not being one to sit on this direction, I scheduled the first Warrior School for the first Tuesday in January. I contacted the two women who readily agreed to be a part. Each week, I wrote a chapter, which I would then teach at the next class. When I completed the seventh chapter, Weapons of Warfare, I knew the study had concluded. I had a couple of guest ministers come in and we prayed over and laid hands on the two warriors—commissioning them and setting them forth. In a couple of months, I held the second Warrior School and since then, subsequent Warrior Schools.

WHY WARRIOR SCHOOL?

God wants us to be equipped. He wants us to be victorious. He certainly gets no glory when any of His children are defeated. Unfortunately, many Christians do not know the Word of God (the Spirit sword). We are spiritually

ignorant. In Hosea 4:6, God told Hosea, *"My people are destroyed for lack of knowledge."*

Warrior School contains the truths God wants us to know to be a victorious warrior through our Lord Jesus Christ! Let's dig in...

Section I

Identity

CHAPTER ONE

RELATIONSHIP

Before we can talk about our identity, we must talk about our relationship with Jesus Christ that gives us our identity in God.

Contrary to the popular saying, "We are all children of God," we are not. Yes, it is true that we are all creations of God, but we are only His children through our relationship with Jesus Christ. We get this truth from several scriptures:

> *"But as many as received Him, to them He gave the right to become children of God, to those who believe in His name* (Jesus)*:"* (John 1:12) (emphasis mine).

> *"For you are all sons of God through faith in Christ Jesus"* (Galatians 3:26).

This clearly shows us that we have the "right to become" the children of God when we believe in Jesus. Those who do NOT believe that Jesus is the only begotten Son of the Most High Living God are NOT children of God. Thankfully, this scripture also shows us this can simply be rectified by believing in Jesus Christ.

Not only have we become children of God through Jesus Christ, but we are now part of His Body, the church of the Lord Jesus Christ.

> *"For we are members of His body, of His flesh and of His bones"* (Ephesians 5:30).

Christ gave Himself for us:

> *"...Christ also loved the church and gave Himself for her,"* (Ephesians 5:25).

Christ satisfies and cleanses us (the church):

> *"that He might sanctify and cleanse her with the washing of water by the word,"* (Ephesians 5:26).

Christ wants to present us (the church) gloriously:

> *"that He might present her to Himself a glorious church..."* (Ephesians 5:27).

Christ wants us (the church) to be holy and without blemish:

> *"...not having spot or wrinkle or any such thing, but that she should be holy and without blemish"* (Ephesians 5:27).

Clearly, the church being glorious is the work of Christ—not the work of the flesh. He has done the hardest work! We can't take away our spots, wrinkles and blemishes nor make ourselves holy. We don't crucify our flesh as this was already done with Christ:

> *"I have been crucified with Christ; it is no longer I who live, but Christ lives in me; and the life which I now live in the flesh I live by faith in the Son of God, who loved me and gave Himself for me"* (Galatians 2:20).

More than likely, if you are reading this book, you are a Christian. If you are not, this wonderful life is for you.

> *"For God so loved the world that He gave His only begotten Son, that WHOEVER believes in Him should not perish but have everlasting life. For God did not send His Son into the world to condemn the world, but that the world through Him might be saved"* (John 3:16-17) (emphasis mine).

That invitation is for anyone who will believe. Will you? If so, you can say this prayer out loud:

> "Jesus, I receive the love of the Father and the invitation for everlasting life by believing that You are my Savior. I confess that You have washed away my sins and You are my Lord. Holy Spirit, my desire is to repent (turn away) from my sinful actions. Transform me. Change my thoughts. Put a watch over my lips and actions. I want a life transformed by Your power—not just a life of manipulated behavior modification. Thank You for giving Your life for me so that I could reign in life and be with You forever. Amen."

Welcome to the Kingdom!

Chapter Two

Identity Crisis

It would be great to start our Christian journey knowing exactly what being a Christian means. Here's a clue: just as we came to Christ by revelation and faith, that is exactly how the rest of our walk with Him will be—by revelation and faith.

When first saved, joy and freedom come with the revelation that we are now a child of God, and we have eternal life! It does not take long for all of that to be challenged by the enemy, circumstances, friends, and family. (Note: this is not in a set order!)

Yet, not continuing in faith and revelation can get us sidetracked into a "religious" lifestyle that is dull, legalistic, passive, powerless, predictable, and boring. Many people try to live like what they thought a Christian was before they got saved. This causes them to "act" like a Christian from a sinner's perspective. It's mere behavior modification! That is a life stifling the joy of the Lord, the Holy Spirit, and the revelation of Who He is and who we now are.

Let's begin to look at our identity as a child of the Most High God. This will supersede our "dead" ideas about Christianity and set us free to live a life of joy, overcoming and unbelievable peace in every situation.

Romans 12:2 says:

> *"And do not be conformed to this world, but be transformed by the renewing of your mind…"*

The Christian life is one of continually renewing our minds through the Holy Spirit. We are being assimilated to have the mind of Christ so we think and therefore act like citizens of the Kingdom of God. We don't just add Jesus to our current lifestyle but are now in the transformation process of being citizens of God's kingdom.

WE HAVE AN IDENTITY CRISIS!

Is it possible that Christians have an identity crisis? If so, is this a small, insignificant thing? Yes, we can have an identity crisis, and NO it is absolutely not a small, insignificant thing. If we do not know who we are, then we will not walk in the dominion, authority and power God meant for us to have. If we do not know our identity through Christ, then someone or something, even our circumstances, will give us our identity.

Could it be true that the church, the Body of the Lord Jesus Christ, has been deceived and we do not know who we are as CHRISTians? Because we don't know who we are, has it allowed a door to be opened for a demonic spirit? While the world debates and CHRISTians are confused, this spirit wreaks havoc and runs rampant in our culture throwing too many into an identity crisis—and not just CHRISTians.

What is one of the crises the world is currently in? People don't know if they are male or female. Men think that by cutting off body parts they can change their DNA and have babies. Women think that by adding synthetic hormones, growing hair and adding body parts they can be men.

"I will praise You, for I am fearfully and wonderfully made; Marvelous are Your works, And that my soul knows very well" (Psalm 139:14).

If CHRISTians do not lead, a void is created and someone or something else will. When this happens, it is never good. When CHRISTians walk in their God-ordained places, filled with truth and the love of God, we can affect every area of culture—media, economy, government, arts/entertainment, religion, education, and family.

TRUTH

Truth. Is it possible that not everyone wants to hear it? We only need to read the gospels to see how Jesus, who not only had truth, but was truth, was hated and challenged by the religious people—the very ones He came to save. Then they hated His truth so much, they conspired and then murdered Him. Obviously, not everyone wants to hear truth—especially when it exposes them.

It takes courage to step into the places God opens for us, but just as the disciples did, we must pray for BOLDNESS! We see examples over and over in the Scripture:

- David had to have courage to face Goliath.
- Joseph had to have courage to go from prison to the palace.
- Esther had to have courage to go uninvited before the king.
- Elijah had to have courage to face the prophets of Baal.
- The three Hebrew children had to have courage not to bow before the king's idol and face the fiery furnace.
- Daniel and the den of lions, etc. etc.

If we are not courageous enough to step up, then we leave a void. We have to know WHO we are in God and the calling He has placed upon each of us.

TWO KINGDOMS

There are two kingdoms: the Kingdom of God (light) and the kingdom of darkness. When we die, we go to Heaven or hell. There is no place of neutrality. If we, as the Body of the Lord Jesus Christ, absent ourselves from any area of culture, then we give permission for the kingdom of darkness to rule.

WHO AM I?

Isn't that the $64,000 question? Generations have struggled with this very question. Because man has been ignorant of his identity, it has allowed despicable, tyrannical people to imprison, limit and destroy good people. It is sadly funny because the tyrants are usually people who are less in number that can corral numbers greater than themselves by two measures: fear and ignorance. Remember the story of the children of Israel? The Egyptians put the children of Israel in bondage because they were greater in number than the Egyptians:

> *"…And they were in dread of the children of Israel"*
> (Exodus 1:12).

Thank God, the opposite is also true as it only takes one person used by God to set people and nations free:

- ➢ Moses was raised in the house of Pharoah but was the deliverer for the children of Israel. (Exodus)
- ➢ Remember David and Goliath? (I Samuel 17)
- ➢ Look at Sampson. (Judges 13-16)
- ➢ God took Gideon with 32,000 men and whittled them down to 300 to defeat the Philistines. (Judges 7)

Of course, the ultimate victory is by our Savior, Jesus Christ! His victory is not only for the generation in which He lived, but for every generation reaching back to Adam and going forward to the last man and woman to be born on the face of the earth. This is with whom we now have eternal life.

WHERE DO WE FIND IDENTITY?

We find our identity in our Creator, God. We know our identity because He tells us what it is. He bought it for us at a great price and then He gave it to us. It's available to anyone. All we need to do is easily receive it by faith. Easily because it's simple, not because it is not challenging.

Where does God tell us about our identity? God tells us about our identity in the Bible. The Bible is God's Word speaking to us. It is relevant to us and to every generation. It is not a "religious" book that we read out of "religious duty," but the Bible is where God reveals Himself to us—whether under the Old Covenant, which has passed away, or the New Covenant, which we live under since the death and resurrection of the perfect lamb, His Son, Jesus Christ.

A CHRISTIAN

Salvation will be laid out again and again through this first section. Why? Because we get saved by believing in the Lord Jesus Christ, but then, sometimes, we are told over and over and over how we've missed the mark. This can cause us to "think" that maybe we aren't saved and yes, our enemy, the accuser of the brethren, will jump on that bandwagon and tell us and question us repeatedly by saying things like:

> "And you call yourself a Christian?!"
> "A Christian wouldn't act that way!"

Hear the "tsk, tsk, tsk" and see the wagging finger? Recognize the accusations of a religious spirit.

Spoiler alert: for those who don't already know, Christians act all kinds of ways and yes, they are still Christians.

MENTAL ASSENT VS. REVELATION

The revelation of our salvation and all that Jesus Christ has done for us needs to be settled in our hearts forever! We have heard truths that we think we believe, but to which we are only mentally assenting and not putting into practice. If we aren't putting truths into practice, then we do not believe them. We all know the truth that brushing our teeth promotes good oral hygiene and helps stop tooth decay and cavities. Even though this is truth, if it is not put into practice, the truth doesn't help us and our teeth will rot.

For example, we know reading the Bible is good, but never opening the Bible or never hearing it preached does us no good. The Bible is not a "magic" book. It sits on thousands of nightstands or in drawers and does no one any good UNTIL faith is applied.

Remember when you learned your multiplication tables?

$2 \times 2 = 4$
$2 \times 3 = 6$
$2 \times 4 = 8$
$2 \times 5 = 10$
$2 \times 6 = 12$
$2 \times 7 = 14$
$2 \times 8 = 16$
$2 \times 9 = 18$

Next are the 3's, 4's, etc.

Repeating these tables starts out being mental assent. "Yes, that's true." "Yes, that's how it works." $2 \times 2 = 4$, and

we could REPEAT the whole table, but we do not necessarily have the revelation that 2 x 2 = 4. If we do not have the revelation of the 2's, then anything out of order could be confusing. When we have the revelation of the multiplication tables, then we can apply this math at any level. It is unnecessary to have to think through the 2's table to get to 2 x 9 = 18 because we "know" that 2 x 9 = 18, at any time. Because we have the "revelation" of the truth that 2 x 9 = 18, any attempt to introduce any other number conclusion can be disregarded because we have the truth. We know, regardless of whatever "proof" is presented, that 2 x 9 = 18.

Liken this to salvation. If we do not know the revelation of our salvation and have only "facts," then when our enemy comes spewing lies, we might be confused or tempted to believe him. Truth and revelation are what arms us against the lies of the enemy. Not only that, without the revelation of our salvation, once we are saved, we might be trying to live what we "thought" a CHRISTian was when we were a sinner. This is performance and falls way short of the relationship Jesus wants to have with us.

Revelation is not just adding something new to what we know. Sometimes, it requires digging out the old and then building the new. Revelation can be like dominos. The truth of a new revelation affects this and this and this. "Old" or "wrong" facts fall like dominos because so many things are inter-connected. Transformation comes when our minds are renewed. Romans 12:2 tells us so.

Identity is knowing who we are in God and what God says about us.

BASIC TRUTH

We are loved! This is a truth we must know and believe from the core of our being. From the very beginning of creation, our enemy has challenged this truth. In the Garden, Adam and Eve met with God in the cool of the day. Imagine God partnering with His creation. Adam named the animals and God accepted it. He told them they could eat from every tree of the Garden, except for two: the tree of life and the tree of the knowledge of good and evil. (Notice this was not just evil knowledge, but good knowledge, as well.) Somehow, the serpent was able to deceive Eve with the thought and the suspicion that God was withholding some very important information from them. This probably did not happen over the course of a few days, but over a period of time. Imagine meeting with God in person every day in the Garden, but even so, Eve began to believe the words of the serpent over the words of God. She traded relationship for knowledge—misleading, false information.

Satan even tried it on Jesus in the wilderness temptations saying, "If you are the Son of God..." We cannot naively believe that because he tried this on Eve and even Jesus, he won't try it on us. If, from the beginning, the enemy maligned and questioned the love of God, it is still a "go-to" strategy for him because he is not creative nor does he have revelation to try something new. He can only use the same tricks and deceptions repeatedly. If we are not confident in God's love for us, those strategies might deceive us. It does not matter how long we have been a CHRISTian, Satan will question God's love for us and our identity in Him again and again. Sadly, we sometimes fall prey to this lie over and over.

Even though Adam failed, Jesus did not! Even though Adam and Eve fell in the most beautiful, perfect garden, Jesus (the 2nd Adam) did not fall in the barren wilderness. Here is more good news: even though Eve was deceived and Adam took freely, God covered them in bloody skins—forgiving them both! Don't you love that?

Everything God does for us—answered prayer, healing, provision, protection, wisdom, guidance, etc.—is because He loves us. Isn't that the whole reason He sent Jesus? *"For God so loved the world that He gave…"* (John 3:16). If we are made in His likeness, which we are, and if we are being made like Jesus, which we are, then love is the basis from which we live, think and operate. After all, God doesn't just have love, He IS love.

We are loved. God does everything through love. That is who He is—not just what He has. John 3:16 tells us that because He loved the world, He sent His only Son to suffer and die for us. Romans 5:8 tells us that while we were still sinners—not when we cleaned up or repented—Christ died for us. God saves us because He loves us. He provides for us because He loves us. He heals us because He loves us. He has callings and destiny for us because He loves us.

When we hear "Warrior School," it's easy to imagine serious soldiers out doing serious harm. This is true regarding the spiritual warfare against our enemy because we are sober and vigilant (I Peter 5:8) since our enemy wants to steal, kill and destroy us (John 10:10). However, our calling toward others is a calling of love. Our calling is to deliver, heal and minister.

So, what is my identity as a CHRISTian? Because I believe in the Lord Jesus Christ as my Savior, I am a CHRISTian. I am a blood-bought, child of the Most High God. I am part of a chosen generation, a royal priesthood, a holy nation, and I am one of His special people.

Chapter Three

Salvation

THE STORY OF THE BROWNS AND SMITHS

Let me tell a fictional story. Albert Brown is a despicable, wicked person. He has raised his family in his footsteps. He has a wife, Tess, and four children, two boys and two girls: Jr., Bubba, Sissy, and Opal. The boys, Jr. and Bubba, are drug runners and bootleggers. Rumor has it that a couple of people who have dealt with them have gone missing, but no one can or will provide evidence Jr. or Bubba were involved. Their mother runs a prostitution ring. The girls not only help run the prostitution ring with their mother, but traffic adults and children for slavery and theft. They have run on the wrong side of the law in their town for as long as anyone can remember.

Across town, the Smith family is totally the opposite of the Browns. Bob and Candy Smith are loving, kind and gracious not only to their family, but to everyone they know. Their children, Robert and Samantha, have only known natural love and security through their parents and through their own personal relationships with Jesus Christ.

Opal Brown goes off to college. Against all odds and to everyone's surprise, she has an encounter with Jesus Christ and her life is totally changed. She is radically transformed. As any good romance story would have it, Robert Smith is at the same school and falls in love with Opal and they get married. Opal is no longer Opal Brown, but Opal Smith.

She is almost thrown into a tailspin with the change in her life. Not only is she a newlywed but is a newlywed Christian married to another Christian. It is so different from the narcissistic, unlawful household in which she was raised. Robert lavishes her with unconditional love, support and security because that's the only thing he knows, both naturally and spiritually. Doesn't this sound great? Truly, it is profound.

Do you think Opal would introduce herself now as Opal Brown Smith? Everyone in her hometown has heard of Opal Brown—and not in a good way. Why would she want to keep her identity tied to the Browns now that she is a Smith? Not only has her name changed (as well as her life since she came to Christ), but the name her children will bear is good—not one to be shunned or disdained.

Wouldn't Opal want to distance herself from the Browns as much as possible? Would she want people to first think of her as a Brown—a drunkard, drug runner, murderer, thief, fraud, and possibly, prostitute—getting that picture in their mind, and then they have doubt she could truly be a Smith—a true, manifesting Christian who is generous, loving and kind?

Make this story personal. Why do we, as Christians, identify as sinners? Why do we think, and therefore say, "I'm just a sinner saved by grace?" Why do we want to give the devil credit for our sin before ever crediting God for our glorious salvation and gift of righteousness?

WE **WERE** SINNERS (past tense). **NOW** (present tense), we are saved, redeemed children of THE loving, gentle, kind, merciful, trustworthy, just, powerful, and forgiving Father! Instead of SINners, we are now CHRISTians!!!

The phrase, "I'm just a sinner saved by grace," sounds like condemnation. "Remember where you came from!" "Know your place!" What's the danger? In Matthew 13, Jesus could do no mighty works in His hometown because of their unbelief. Imagine, Jesus, the SON OF GOD filled with the Holy Ghost and power, could do no mighty works because of the unbelief of His former neighbors and towns people. What caused their unbelief? They remembered who He WAS. Read their reasoning:

> *"Is this not the carpenter's son? Is not His mother called Mary? And His brothers James, Joses, Simon, and Judas? And His sisters, are they not all with us? Where then did this Man get all these things?"'* (Matthew 13:55-56).

Being reminded of who we WERE keeps us powerless. That's what religion does—it keeps us passive and powerless.

BLOOD CONSCIOUSNESS VS. SIN CONSCIOUSNESS

Unfortunately, sin consciousness is more prevalent than blood of Jesus consciousness. What does that mean? Basically, we are more conscious of the demonic actions of our fallen nature rather than the victory won by the shed blood of our Lord and Savior. Jesus is the only begotten Son of God who gave His life for us and when we accepted Him, we became a new creation! **We are not just forgiven—we are made a new creation!**

When Jesus died, His shed blood, His sacrifice went all the way back to Adam and all the way forward to the last man/woman who will ever be born. That is powerful. There is no "new" sin that has not been covered by the shed blood of Jesus.

Let's break this down with an example of stain consciousness vs. cleanser consciousness.

STAIN CONSCIOUSNESS VS. CLEANSER CONSCIOUSNESS

I have a white tablecloth and serve spaghetti to my family. As always, spaghetti sauce gets on the white tablecloth. The tablecloth is now stained and possibly ruined. However, I have a stain remover. I apply the stain remover and wash the tablecloth. When I take it out of the washing machine, the cloth is spotless!

I can have several reactions:

1) I rejoice that I have found a powerful cleanser. I can have spaghetti as much as I want. OR…
2) I rejoice that I have a powerful cleanser, but feel the need to point out where the spot "was," even though it can no longer be seen. OR…
3) I stop serving spaghetti or anything with a tomato base, or mustard, or grape juice (the list is endless). OR…
4) I cover the tablecloth with plastic because the cleanser may have worked once, but it doesn't mean it will work again if I purposely spill something that stains. I do not have confidence in the cleanser, so I have to take action.

Which is your option? Which is the way you believe and practice your salvation?

THE BLOOD OF JESUS

Under the Old Covenant, God put in place the offering of bulls and goats as a blood sacrifice to COVER their sins. When the children of Israel brought those sacrificial animals, God honored the sacrifice and they were forgiven. God honored the covenant and His system worked.

We can even look back to the Garden of Eden and see how God used a blood sacrifice for Adam and Eve. What happened when Adam and Eve ate the fruit of the forbidden tree of the knowledge of good and evil? Adam and Eve covered themselves with salad makings—leaves. God killed animals to get their skins and then covered Adam and Eve smearing them with those bloody skins—covering their sin.

Romans 3:23 says:

"for ALL have sinned and fall short of the glory of God,"
(emphasis mine).

Adam and Eve were not in a fallen state when they were created. They fell out of the glory causing them to have a fallen nature. This is one reason they didn't know they were naked—they were covered in the glory. Now that they didn't have the glory for covering, God provided (IN THEIR SINFUL STATE) coverings to protect them.

Ponder this: when we fall from grace, we do not fall into sin. When we fall from grace, we fall into the law. We either live under grace or under the law. Grace is receiving what Jesus did for us. Law is where we must pay the penalty for our sins. Let's choose grace.

When Jesus came, offered up His life and shed His blood, it WASHED AWAY sin, it did not just cover sin.

"For it is not possible that the blood of bulls and goats could take away sins" (Hebrews 10:4).

"how much more shall the blood of Christ, who through the eternal Spirit offered Himself without spot to God, cleanse your conscience from dead works to serve the living God?"
(Hebrews 9:14).

"But if we walk in the light as He is in the light, we have fellowship with one another, and the blood of Jesus Christ His Son cleanses us from all sin" (I John 1:7).

"...To Him who loved us and washed us from our sins in His own blood" (Revelation 1:5).

"...without shedding of blood there is no remission" (Hebrews 9:22).

Hebrews 9:22 is a present tense verb, *"without <u>shedding of blood</u>,"* If we do not partake of the blood that WAS shed for us, there is no blood being shed for us now.

The problem with the blood of bulls and goats was it only "covered" sin and didn't wash away sin permanently. The blood of bulls and goats was not perfect and was only temporary—it was only good until the next time someone sinned. **The blood of Jesus IS NOT like the blood of bulls and goats! It is not temporary!**

Therefore, what Jesus has done is FAR GREATER than what sin could do. Sin IS NOT GREATER than the blood of Jesus. It DID NOT stop Jesus from offering Himself and He DID NOT wait until man was repentant and sinless to come!

"But God demonstrates His own love toward us, in that <u>while we were still sinners</u>, Christ died for us. <u>Much more</u> then, <u>having now been justified by His blood</u>, we shall be saved from wrath through Him. For <u>if when we were enemies</u> we were reconciled to God through the death of His Son, <u>much more, having been reconciled, we shall be saved</u> by His life" (Romans 5:8-10) (emphasis mine).

Ponder this: under the old covenant, a sacrifice was required when one had sinned. The sacrifice was then examined by the priest to make sure it did not have any spot or blemish. Therefore, when a man brought a lamb to be sacrificed for him and his family to cover their sin, the priest didn't examine the man. He knew the man was sinful. He examined the lamb. It was the lamb that had to be perfect and spotless—not the man. When we come to God, He examines our Lamb. Is our Lamb perfect and spotless? OH YES, HE IS!!!!

SIN VS. SIN NATURE

Adam was not created with a sinful nature but fell after he willingly ate the fruit of the forbidden tree. God saved Adam and Eve by putting them out of the Garden so they would not eat of the tree of life and stay sinful, therefore doomed to die and not have eternal life. Every person after Adam was born with a sinful nature.

The purpose of Jesus being born to a virgin was not only a sign as prophesied in the Book of Isaiah, but it was much more. In the natural, the blood comes to a baby from the father. The Son of God could not have man's blood or a sinful nature. He had to be perfect and sinless, or His blood would not have been accepted by the Father as the sacrifice for all who would believe and receive it—making them a new creation. That new creation does away with our sinful nature. We might sin, but it doesn't make us a "sinner."

Let's redefine "sinner." Usually, the reference to a sinner is one who sins. That is not a good definition. What if we defined a duck as one who quacks? I can quack. Everybody can quack, quack. Does that make us ducks? No, of course not. A "sinner" is one without Jesus.

Let's be clear: <u>sin is wrong</u>. We should run from it and shun it. We should not be participating in it, but if we do sin, we have not fallen from being a Christian. We are a new

creation. Once we are a CHRISTian, sinning doesn't make us a "sinner." It just makes us a CHRISTian who needs to repent (change direction), receive the forgiveness of Jesus and ask the Holy Spirit to watch what we say, direct our steps and give us wisdom. We need our thinking transformed so we can be renewed.

"...be transformed by the renewing of your mind, that you may prove what is that good and acceptable and perfect will of God" (Romans 12:2).

Example: If you are married and commit adultery, IT IS WRONG! Yes, you need to confess it to your spouse. Yes, you need to make it right and not participate in adultery anymore. Yes, you need to repent (change your mind and direction), but because you committed adultery, this does not make you un-married! This is the same way with being a CHRISTian. Sinning doesn't make you not a CHRISTian. (This is not an excuse to continue in sin.) If you are sinning, REPENT (turn away from it) and ask the Holy Spirit to help you!

"...Walk in the Spirit, and you shall not fulfill the lust of the flesh" (Galatians 5:16).

Now, back to the adultery scenario. If adultery is confessed to the spouse, but adultery is continued, then that was confession, NOT REPENTANCE. Repentance is a change of direction. **Metanoia** is the Greek word for repentance. It means to think differently or afterwards to reconsider, change direction. If sinning continues, there has not been true repentance, just confession.

WHAT DO WE BELIEVE? (This will be discussed more in Section 2)

Do we believe we are saved because we stopped sinning? This is not scriptural. We are saved because we believe Jesus Christ is the Son of God and His blood has washed away our sins because His sacrifice was accepted by the Father! Yes, we should absolutely turn away from sin, but our salvation is based on us believing in Jesus, not in our ability to stop being sinful!

JESUS CHRIST is the only begotten Son of God. The rest of us are adopted.

> *"Yet all of this was so that he would redeem and set free all those held hostage to the law so that we would receive our freedom and a full legal adoption as his children"* (Galatians 4:5 TPT).

> *"For it was always in his perfect plan to adopt us as his delightful children, through our union with Jesus, the Anointed One, so that his tremendous love that cascades over us would glorify his grace—for <u>the same love he has for the Beloved, Jesus, he has for us</u>. And this unfolding plan brings him great pleasure!"* (Ephesians 1:5-6 TPT) (emphasis mine).

Doesn't that enlarge your mind and increase your love for Him to think that God has the same love for you that He has for Jesus?! How is that even possible?

NASTY LITTLE BOY

One of my daughters went on a missions trip to Nicaragua while she was in high school. They were going to visit the city dump where it was estimated 150,000 people lived. As an

American in a first world country, that is almost inconceivable, but God gave me a word picture regarding this.

Imagine going to the dump and seeing a nasty little boy. He is obviously an orphan or a child left to his own charge. He is about eight-years-old. His hair is matted and his clothes are grimy and tattered. Who knows the last time he bathed or the last time he brushed his teeth? He has snot trails coming down from his nose and he has tear tracks that have been smeared on his face. The tear tracks are certainly from the grit and grime in his eyes as he has hardened himself not to even allow any vulnerabilities to show or he might be devoured in this unforgiving, dog-eat-dog hell hole. Yet, there's something about this little guy.

He kicks and screams and cusses like a sailor. He uses words never heard in polite society, but they roll off his tongue from their frequent use in his limited vocabulary. He even spits at anyone who comes near. Yet, there's something about this little guy.

Imagine your heart goes out to him. You want to bring him to your home. You want to get him bathed and put clean clothes on him. You want to give him a warm, clean, soft bed and feed him hot, nutritious meals. You wonder if he would enjoy a trip to the zoo. How would he act at the beach? You can't ask him because he has no paradigm for those activities to say "yes" or "no." What would he act like if he ate regular meals and he knew he could be his true eight-year-old self instead of acting like a tough guy of 18?

He does nothing to show his interest in you. He again cusses and screams and kicks at you. Yet, there's something about this little guy.

Who is this story about? Is it about the little boy? No, it's about you. The little boy was just being the little boy. It was your love and compassion that went beyond how he acted and what he looked like. It was your love and compassion that wanted to change the situation for him because he probably couldn't think beyond the dump.

That's how God can love us like Jesus—because it's not about us doing anything to earn His love. It's that He is love and He can't help Himself no matter how we act or speak. There's just something about us! *"For God so loved the world…"*

If He loves us at our worst, what could we ever do to make Him love us more? **We are a new creation.**

> *"Therefore, if anyone is in Christ, he is a new creation; old things have passed away; behold, <u>all things</u> have become new"* (II Corinthians 5:17) (emphasis mine).

FAITHFULESS OF JESUS

If we constantly hear about sin, from our own thinking (remember Satan is the accuser of the brethren and he is good at that) or from the religious, who does sin glorify? Sin doesn't glorify Jesus. So, if we let guilt and condemnation have free reign, we will never realize the freedom Christ has brought into our life. This freedom is not just spiritual but is walked out in our physical life. So, basically, if we constantly think about sin, we are meditating on what the devil has done. When we think of our new creation, we are meditating on what Jesus has done. We stand on the faithfulness of Jesus, not our ability to do right.

> *"And when the season of tolerance came to an end, there was only one possible way for God to give away his righteousness and still be true to both his justice and his mercy—to offer up his own Son. So now, because <u>we stand on the faithfulness of Jesus</u>, God declares us righteous in his eyes!"* (Romans 3:26 TPT) (emphasis mine).

In other words, in every situation, we must be conscious that we are a blood-bought child of the Most High God. We may have sinned, but we are not sinners (ones without Jesus). We repent, not to bring our state back to being a CHRISTian, but we repent to change and go in the opposite direction.

SOLIDITY OF OUR SALVATION

When we got saved, we did not just make a "decision" for Christ. If we only made a "decision," then we can always change our mind!

Receiving and entering salvation is an eternal change of our being. Salvation is not fragile, brittle, flighty, or shifting. Salvation is strong, steady and weighty. Salvation was costly. Salvation is not something we walk out by ourselves. Salvation has caused us to be adopted and accepted by God. We are in God's hands and no one can take us out of His hands. Angels walk with us and minister to us. We have the Holy Spirit who never leaves us nor forsakes us. Jesus, the precious and only begotten Son of God, suffered and died on our behalf—to redeem US! God has skin and blood in the game. God has invested in us. He will not let that investment go. Salvation is eternal. (We can't let our enemy, the devil, lie to us and tell us nothing happened!)

> *"Jesus was handed over to be crucified for the forgiveness of our sins and was raised back to life to prove that he had made us right with God!"* (Romans 4:25 TPT).

CATERPILLAR TO BUTTERFLY

Imagine a caterpillar in a chrysalis. Once that caterpillar transforms into a butterfly, it can never be a caterpillar again. It can hang around its old cocoon. It might even go back into the cocoon, BUT IT WILL NEVER be a caterpillar again. Our salvation is that dramatic!

Salvation is an answer to a deep call of God unto the depths of our spirit resurrecting us from eternal darkness, chaos, separation, defeat, and death.

> *"Deep calls unto deep at the noise of Your waterfalls..."*
> (Psalm 42:7).

> *"But you are a chosen generation, a royal priesthood, a holy nation, His own special people, that you may proclaim the praises of Him who called YOU out of darkness into His marvelous light;"* (I Peter 2:9) (emphasis mine).

I AM dead to sin. There has been a reversal. Instead of us being alive to sin and an enemy of God, we are now dead to sin and alive to God.

> *"Likewise you also, reckon yourselves to be dead indeed to sin, but alive to God in Christ Jesus our Lord"* (Romans 6:11).

> *"And you, who once were alienated and enemies in your mind by wicked works, yet now He has reconciled in the body of His flesh through death, to present you holy, and blameless, and above reproach in His sight—"* (Colossians 1:21-22).

I AM a new creation. The unredeemed person with a sin nature that we were is gone.

> *"Therefore, if anyone is in Christ, he is a new creation; old things have passed away; behold, all things have become new"*
> (II Corinthians 5:17).

> *"Through our union with him we have experienced circumcision of heart. <u>All of the guilt and power of sin has been cut away and is now extinct because of what Christ, the</u>*

Anointed One, has accomplished for us. For we've been buried with him into his death. Our 'baptism into death' also means we were raised with him when we believed in God's resurrection power, the power that raised him from death's realm. This 'realm of death' describes our former state, for we were held in sin's grasp. But now, we've been resurrected out of that 'realm of death' never to return, for we are forever alive and forgiven of all our sins! He canceled out every legal violation we had on our record and the old arrest warrant that stood to indict us. He erased it all—our sins, our stained soul—he deleted it all and they cannot be retrieved! Everything we once were in Adam has been placed onto his cross and nailed permanently there as a public display of cancellation"
(Colossians 2:11-14 TPT) (emphasis mine).

"By God's will we have been purified and made holy once and for all through the sacrifice of the body of Jesus, the Messiah! Yet every day priests still serve, ritually offering the same sacrifices again and again—sacrifices that can never take away sin's guilt. But when this Priest had offered the one supreme sacrifice for sin for all time he sat down on a throne at the right hand of God,...And by his one perfect sacrifice he made us perfectly holy and complete for all time!...So if our sins have been forgiven and forgotten, why would we ever need to offer another sacrifice for sin?"
(Hebrews 10:10-12,14,18 TPT) (emphasis mine).

Under the old covenant, the High Priest came into the Holy of Holies once a year representing the children of Israel to God. The High Priest brought the blood of a sacrificial lamb into the Holy of Holies to receive forgiveness. Jesus Christ is our lamb and His blood was not only shed on the earth, but after He died on the cross, He took His blood to the heavenly tabernacle to be accepted by God. Because it was accepted, Jesus stands as our High Priest to present us faultless before the Father forever.

CONVICTION VS. CONDEMNATION

The best way to define this is conviction draws us **to** God while condemnation drives us **away** from God. Here is the bottom line, if we sin and the Holy Spirit leaves us, what kind of God is that? That is when we need God the most!!!! He is not afraid of sin!

"If we confess our sins, He is faithful and just to forgive us our sins and to cleanse us from all unrighteousness" (I John 1:9).

DANCING WITH THE ATTORNEY

Years ago, I worked in an attorney's office. It was a large, corporate law firm. At Christmas, we always had a big luncheon, got off a little early, and sometimes, some of the attorneys and staff would wander over to the hotel across the street and go where they played music and had drinks. I went over one year just to be with everyone.

One of the older attorneys came up and asked me to dance. I said, "I didn't know how to dance," and thought that would cause him to turn away. Not so. He said, "Let me show you how."

He took me in his arms and held me firmly. He was so confident and such a good dancer. He led me beautifully. I felt like I had taken dance lessons for years. I could tell the direction he was going and was able to relax and enjoy the time.

Weird picture? Not really. Imagine you've missed it. You've messed up. You are embarrassed and think you are out of God's "good graces." Then, along comes the Holy Spirit and says, "Let me show you how." Instead of pushing you away, He draws you closer and says, "Hold close to Me. I know the way to go!"

This is the Holy Spirit that never leaves us—even when we've sinned. He is the One who leads us back. He is the one who comforts us as He is our Comforter. He is the one who teaches us as He leads us into all truth.

After all, if we can do it on our own, why do we need Him? That is the religious, lying, legal system the world lives under—doing everything in their own strength and self-effort.

We have the Holy Spirit who leads, guides, empowers, and comforts us. He doesn't leave us when the going gets rough and when we need it, He draws us near to show us the way.

CONFESSING AND REPENTING

We don't just confess. We also repent. Many people confess—listing their sins, but never repent, which is changing our minds and turning away from those sinful deeds. The Holy Spirit leads us and empowers us to turn.

The Holy Spirit doesn't point out our faults. Who wants to be around someone who is always pointing out where we've failed and fallen short? He is our Teacher and Comforter. He is constantly drawing us to the Father. This is why we came to Jesus in the first place—the Holy Spirit was drawing us. He is always wooing hearts to the Father—especially the unsaved and those whose hearts have grown cold.

> *"Do the riches of his extraordinary kindness make you take him for granted and despise him? Haven't you experienced how kind and understanding he has been to you? Don't mistake his tolerance for acceptance. Do you realize that all the wealth of his extravagant kindness is meant to melt your heart and lead you into repentance?"* (Romans 2:4 TPT).

Jesus said:

"And when He (The Holy Spirit) *has come, He will convict the world of sin, and of righteousness, and of judgment:"*
(John 16:8) (emphasis mine).

Read that verse again. The Holy Spirit convicts the world of sin. He convicted us of our sin, which is why we became a CHRISTian! He doesn't convict the world of their righteousness because they have none! He convicts us of our righteousness. He doesn't say:

"Oh, what a sinner you are."
"A Christian wouldn't talk like that."
"You are always missing it."
"A Christian should be loving!"

Those, my friend, are the words of a religious spirit. The Holy Spirit convicts us of our righteousness like this:

"You are a child of the Most High God."
"You have rivers of living water flowing through you."
"His love flows through you."
"Speak words of life and love to others like He speaks to you."
"Don't you remember that you are the temple of the Most High God?"

CONSCIENCE

God gives everyone a conscience. That conscience has right/wrong written in it (the law). Once we are saved, we no longer live by our conscience. We now have the Spirit of God that leads us and guides us.

> *"And you, being dead in your trespasses and the uncircumcision of your flesh, He has made alive together with Him, having forgiven you all trespasses, having wiped out the handwriting of requirements that was against us which was contrary to us. And He has taken it out of the way, having nailed it to the cross"* (Colossians 2:13-14).

What was nailed to the cross? The law that condemned us!

Is sin wrong? Unequivocally, YES! Is it acceptable, winked at or disregarded? Absolutely not! **BUT** the blood of Jesus is greater and more powerful!

> *"And the gift is not like that which came through the one [Adam] who sinned. For the judgment which came from one offense resulted in condemnation, but the free gift which came from many offenses resulted in justification. For if by the one man's offense [Adam] death reigned through the one, MUCH MORE those who receive abundance of grace and of the gift of righteousness will reign in life through the One, JESUS CHRIST)"* (Romans 5:16-17) (emphasis mine).

Don't you love this? The gift is greater than the offense. What Jesus did, redeeming us, is greater than the fall that Adam caused.

A DEFINING REVELATION

The first time I heard this next statement, I said, "Now, wait a minute," but then once it sunk in past my religious mindset, I said, "Of course." Take a deep breath…

There is one thing and one thing only that will send us to hell. It is not believing in and receiving the Lord Jesus Christ! Everything else is forgivable!

I'm not saved because I quit sinning. I'm saved because I believe in the Lord Jesus Christ! My sin didn't stop me from being saved and it doesn't keep me from staying saved. After I'm saved and because I'm transformed, I can stop sinning.

> *"But God demonstrates His own love toward us, in that <u>while we were still sinners</u>, Christ died for us"* (Romans 5:8) (emphasis mine).

> *"For God so loved the world that He gave His only begotten Son, that whoever <u>believes in Him</u> should not perish but have everlasting life"* (John 3:16) (emphasis mine).

> *"that if you confess with your mouth the Lord Jesus and <u>believe in your heart</u> that God has raised Him from the dead, you will be saved"* (Romans 10:9) (emphasis mine).

If we have believed in our heart and confessed with our mouth that Jesus is Lord, then we are GLORIOUSLY, SOLIDLY, WONDERFULLY, AND ETERNALLY SAVED! The Bible tells us so!

Chapter Four

Identity Markers

Now that we have discussed our identity, let's apply that identity and be aware of Identity Markers (IMs) according to what has been written to us in the Bible. Let's dive in and see the identity God has given us.

I AM righteous. Why is "I AM" capitalized? Because that is what God said His name was when talking to Moses. David Schoch, a minister friend of ours used to say that "I AM" meant God is whatever we need Him to be whenever we need Him to be it.

We include His name in our confession. God has made all these things true. God is always present. "I AM" is present tense. What we say matters.

> *"Death and life are in the power of the tongue, And those who love it will eat its fruit"* (Proverbs 18:21).

We live in a death culture. Listen to how we talk:

> "I'm scared to death."
> "I'm dying to go there."
> "I died laughing."
> "It's to die for!"

What are we saying—death words or life words? Is our conversation and our faith for life or death?

We don't even get saved without confession:

> *"that if you confess with your mouth the Lord Jesus and believe in your heart that God has raised Him from the dead, you will be saved"* (Romans 10:9).

His righteousness is gifted to us when we receive Jesus Christ.

> *"Now, we realize that everything the law says is addressed to those who are under its authority. This is for two reasons: So that every excuse will be silenced, with no boasting of innocence. And so that the entire world will be held accountable to God's standards. For by the merit of observing the law <u>no one</u> earns the status of being declared righteous before God, for it is the law that fully exposes and unmasks the reality of sin. But now, independently of the law, the righteousness of God is tangible and brought to light through Jesus, the Anointed One. This is the righteousness that the Scriptures prophesied would come. It is God's righteousness made visible <u>through the faithfulness of Jesus Christ</u>. And now all who believe in him receive that gift. For there is really no difference between us, for we all have sinned and are in need of the glory of God. Yet through his powerful declaration of acquittal, God freely gives away his righteousness. His gift of love and favor now cascades over us, all because Jesus, the Anointed One, has liberated us from the guilt, punishment, and power of sin! Jesus' God-given destiny was to be the sacrifice to take away sins, and now he is our mercy seat because of his death on the cross. We come to him for mercy, for God has made a provision for us to be <u>forgiven by faith in the sacred blood of Jesus</u>. This is the perfect demonstration of God's justice, because until now, he had been so patient—holding back his justice out of his tolerance for us. So he covered over the sins of those who lived prior to Jesus' sacrifice. And when the season of tolerance came to an end, there was only one possible way for God to give away his*

righteousness and still be true to both his justice and his mercy—to offer up his own Son. So now, <u>because we stand on the faithfulness of Jesus</u>, God declares us righteous in his eyes! Where, then, is there room for boasting? Do our works bring God's acceptance? Not at all! It was not our works of keeping the law but our faith in his finished work that makes us right with God. So our conclusion is this: God's wonderful declaration that we are righteous in his eyes can only come when we put our faith in Christ, and not in keeping the law" (Romans 3:19-28 TPT) (emphasis mine).

I LOVE THIS SCRIPTURE: *"because we stand on the faithfulness of Jesus."* It's not our faithfulness or ability to live sin free, but the faithfulness of Jesus.

How can we be righteous when we know we have been so sinful? Here's a question: did Jesus commit any sin? NO! Then how could He die for our sins? He was not sinful. How could He pay the price? It's simple. He "took" our sins, our guilt and our shame upon Himself. This is the same way we "take" the gift of His righteousness upon us. Therefore, one of our Identify Markers is "I AM righteous."

I AM saved and have eternal life. We have eternal life once we receive Jesus—now, not waiting until we die. Because once we die, it is too late to get eternal life.

"For God so loved the world that He gave His only begotten Son, that whoever <u>believes in Him</u> should not perish but have everlasting life" (John 3:16) (emphasis mine).

"that if you confess with your mouth the Lord Jesus and <u>believe in your heart</u> that God has raised Him from the dead, you will be saved" (Romans 10:9) (emphasis mine).

I AM full of flowing, living water.

> "He who <u>believes in Me</u>, as the Scripture has said, out of his heart will flow rivers of living water" (John 7:38) (emphasis mine).

I AM a child of the living God!

> "But as many as received Him, to them He gave the right to become children of God, to <u>those who believe in His name</u>:" (John 1:12) (emphasis mine).

I AM saved and have eternal life.
I AM full of living, flowing water.
I AM a child of the living God.
I AM a new creation.

Let's list some additional Identity Markers.

I AM loved—God so loved ME.

> "For here is the way God loved the world—he gave his only, unique Son as a gift. So now everyone who believes in him will never perish but experience everlasting life" (John 3:16 TPT).

I AM supplied according to the riches of God, not according to my need.

> "And my God shall supply all your need according to His riches in glory by Christ Jesus" (Philippians 4:19).

I AM dead to sin, but alive to God.

> "Likewise you also, reckon yourselves to be dead indeed to sin, but alive to God in Christ Jesus our Lord" (Romans 6:11).

Read this in The Passion Translation:

"So let it be the same way with you! Since you are now joined with him, <u>you must continually view yourselves as dead and unresponsive to sin's appeal</u> while living daily for God's pleasure in union with Jesus, the Anointed One" (Romans 6:11 TPT) (emphasis mine).

I AM accepted by Jesus.

"to the praise of the glory of His grace, by which He made us accepted in the Beloved" (Ephesians 1:6).

I AM redeemed.
I AM adopted.

"But when the fullness of the time had come, God sent forth His Son, born of a woman, born under the law, to redeem those who were under the law, that we might receive the adoption as sons" (Galatians 4:4-5).

I AM a chosen one.

"And you are among the chosen ones who are called to belong to Jesus, the Anointed One" (Romans 1:6 TPT).

I AM His darling.

"…To those who were rejected and not my people, I will say to them: 'You are mine.' And to those who were unloved I will say: 'You are my darling'" (Romans 9:25-26 TPT).

True humility is not believing what we think or feel about ourselves, but it is believing what the Father says about us!

I AM dead to sin. There has been a reversal. Instead of us being alive to sin and an enemy of God, we are now dead to sin and alive to God.

> *"Likewise you also, reckon yourselves to be dead indeed to sin, but alive to God in Christ Jesus our Lord"* (Romans 6:11).

> *"And you, who once were alienated and enemies in your mind by wicked works, yet now He has reconciled in the body of His flesh through death, to present you holy, and blameless, and above reproach in His sight—"* (Colossians 1:21-22).

I AM eternal. We had eternal death, but when we believed in Jesus, our Savior, from and for our sins, we now have eternal life.

> *"For God so loved the world that He gave His only begotten Son, that whoever believes in Him should not perish but have everlasting life"* (John 3:16).

I AM now a citizen of Heaven and a member of the Church of the Firstborn.

> *"By contrast, we have already come near to God in a totally different realm, the Zion-realm, for we have entered the city of the Living God, which is the New Jerusalem in heaven! We have joined the festal gathering of myriads of angels in their joyous celebration! And as members of the church of the Firstborn all our names have been legally registered as citizens of heaven! And we have come before God who judges all, and who lives among the spirits of the righteous who have been made perfect in his eyes!"* (Hebrews 12:22-23 TPT).

I AM blessed. Our sin was imputed to Jesus.

> *"Blessed is the man to whom the LORD shall not impute sin"* (Romans 4:8).

I AM free from the law of sin and death and walk in Spirit-of-life laws!

> *"For the law of the Spirit of life in Christ Jesus has made me free from the law of sin and death"* (Romans 8:2).

> *"...Walk in the Spirit, and you shall not fulfill the lust of the flesh"* (Galatians 5:16).

I AM free. We have been freed from the power of the lesser kingdom to become part of the greater Kingdom of God.

> *"He has delivered us from the power of darkness and conveyed us into the kingdom of the Son of His love, in whom we have redemption through His blood, the forgiveness of sins"* (Colossians 1:13-14).

I AM a new creation. The unredeemed person with a sin nature that we WERE is gone.

> *"Therefore, if anyone is in Christ, he is a new creation; old things have passed away; behold, all things have become new"* (II Corinthians 5:17).

> *"Through our union with him we have experienced circumcision of heart. <u>All of the guilt and power of sin has been cut away and is now extinct because of what Christ, the Anointed One, has accomplished for us.</u> For we've been buried with him into his death. Our 'baptism into death' also means we were raised with him when we believed in God's resurrection power, the power that raised him from death's realm. This 'realm of death' describes <u>our former state</u>, for we were held in sin's grasp. But now, <u>we've been resurrected out of that 'realm of death' never to return, for we are forever alive and forgiven of all our sins! He canceled out every legal violation we had on our record and the old arrest warrant that stood to indict us. He erased it all—our sins, our stained soul—he deleted it all</u>

<u>and they cannot be retrieved</u>! Everything we once were in Adam has been placed onto his cross and <u>nailed permanently there as a public display of cancellation</u>"
(Colossians 2:11-14 TPT) (emphasis mine).

"By God's will we have been purified and made holy <u>once and for all through the sacrifice of the body of Jesus, the Messiah</u>! Yet every day priests still serve, ritually offering the same sacrifices again and again—sacrifices that can never take away sin's guilt. But when this Priest had offered the one supreme sacrifice for sin for all time he sat down on a throne at the right hand of God,…And <u>by his one perfect sacrifice he made us perfectly holy and complete for all time!…So if our sins have been forgiven and forgotten, why would we ever need to offer another sacrifice for sin?</u>"
(Hebrews 10:10-12,14,18 TPT) (emphasis mine).

Assignment: Find Identity Markers in Psalm 91

> "He who dwells in the secret place of the Most High Shall abide under the shadow of the Almighty. I will say of the LORD, 'He is my refuge and my fortress; My God, in Him I will trust.' Surely He shall deliver you from the snare of the fowler And from the perilous pestilence. He shall cover you with His feathers, And under His wings you shall take refuge; His truth shall be your shield and buckler. You shall not be afraid of the terror by night, Nor of the arrow that flies by day, Nor of the pestilence that walks in darkness, Nor of the destruction that lays waste at noonday. A thousand may fall at your side, And ten thousand at your right hand; But it shall not come near you. Only with your eyes shall you look, And see the reward of the wicked. Because you have made the LORD, who is my refuge, Even the Most High, your dwelling place, No evil shall befall you, Nor shall any plague come near your dwelling; For He shall give His angels charge over you, To keep you in all your ways. In their hands they shall bear you up, Lest you dash your foot against a stone. You shall tread upon the lion and the cobra, The young lion and the serpent you shall trample underfoot. 'Because he has set his love upon Me, therefore I will deliver him; I will set him on high, because he has known My name. He shall call upon Me, and I will answer him; I will be with him in trouble; I will deliver him and honor him. With long life I will satisfy him, And show him My salvation'" (Psalm 91:1-16).

_____

_____

_____

_____

_____

Assignment: Find Identity Markers in Psalm 103

"Bless the LORD, O my soul; And all that is within me, bless His holy name! Bless the LORD, O my soul, And forget not all His benefits: Who forgives all your iniquities, Who heals all your diseases, Who redeems your life from destruction, Who crowns you with lovingkindness and tender mercies, Who satisfies your mouth with good things, So that your youth is renewed like the eagle's. The LORD executes righteousness And justice for all who are oppressed. He made known His ways to Moses, His acts to the children of Israel. The LORD is merciful and gracious, Slow to anger, and abounding in mercy. He will not always strive with us, Nor will He keep His anger forever. He has not dealt with us according to our sins, Nor punished us according to our iniquities. For as the heavens are high above the earth, So great is His mercy toward those who fear Him; As far as the east is from the west, So far has He removed our transgressions from us. As a father pities his children, So the LORD pities those who fear Him. For He knows our frame; He remembers that we are dust. As for man, his days are like grass; As a flower of the field, so he flourishes. For the wind passes over it, and it is gone, And its place remembers it no more. But the mercy of the LORD is from everlasting to everlasting On those who fear Him, And His righteousness to children's children, To such as keep His covenant, And to those who remember His commandments to do them. The LORD has established His throne in heaven, And His kingdom rules over all. Bless the LORD, you His angels, Who excel in strength, who do His word, Heeding the voice of His word. Bless the LORD, all you His hosts, You ministers of His, who do His pleasure. Bless the LORD, all His works, In all places of His dominion. Bless the LORD, O my soul!" (Psalm 103:1-22).

Psalm 91 Identity Markers (Cheat Sheet)

I AM a dweller and abide under the shadow of the Almighty.

> (vs. 1) *"He who dwells in the secret place of the Most High Shall abide under the shadow of the Almighty."*

I AM in a refuge and fortress.

> (vs. 2) *"I will say of the Lord, 'He is my refuge and my fortress; My God, in Him I will trust.'"*

I AM delivered.

> (vs. 3) *"Surely He shall deliver you from the snare of the fowler And from the perilous pestilence."*

I AM covered with His feathers.

> (vs. 4) *"He shall cover you with His feathers, And under His wings you shall take refuge;..."*

I have truth. (I have—we can be identified by what we have or don't have—the man who drives that purple car, the woman who owns that beautiful house, the poor man, the homeless person.)

> (vs. 4) *"...His truth shall be your shield and buckler."*

I AM not afraid.

> (vs. 5-8) *"You shall not be afraid of the terror by night, Nor of the arrow that flies by day, Nor of the pestilence that walks in darkness, Nor of the destruction that lays waste at noonday. A thousand may fall at your side, And ten thousand at your*

right hand; But it shall not come near you. Only with your eyes shall you look, And see the reward of the wicked."

I AM safe—no evil shall befall me nor plague come near my dwelling.

(vs. 9-10) *"Because you have made the* LORD, *who is my refuge, Even the Most High, your dwelling place, No evil shall befall you, Nor shall any plague come near your dwelling;"*

I AM under the care of angels.

(vs. 11-13) *"For He shall give His angels charge over you, To keep you in all your ways. In their hands they shall bear you up, Lest you dash your foot against a stone. You shall tread upon the lion and the cobra, The young lion and the serpent you shall trample underfoot."*

I AM delivered and God answers me.

(vs. 14-15) *"Because he has set his love upon Me, therefore I will deliver him; I will set him on high, because he has known My name. He shall call upon Me, and I will answer him;..."*

I AM not alone.

(vs. 15) *"...I will be with him in trouble; I will deliver him and honor him."*

I have long life and He satisfies me.

(vs. 16) "With long life I will satisfy him, And show him My salvation."

List other Identity Markers that mean something to you:

Section II

Belief

Chapter Five

What Do We Believe?

"Jesus said to him, 'If you can believe, all things are possible to him who believes'" (Mark 9:23).

The truths we are studying are for our whole lives. The enemy has no compassion, whether we are young or old. Life is a marathon, not a sprint. We do not "arrive." The just LIVE by faith. It is our way of life.

Is what we believe crucial? Absolutely! If we believe in Jesus, we have eternal life and go to Heaven. If we don't believe in Jesus, we go to hell. What we believe is very important.

Belief is the very foundation of our salvation because we are only saved when we BELIEVE in Jesus Christ as the only begotten Son of God who gave His life as a ransom for our sinful self. We believe that God accepted the blood sacrifice of Jesus for us and every human, from Adam and Eve to the last man or woman to be born. The cross is the punishment for the sin of mankind. Sin caused Jesus to have to hang on that cross. BUT the empty tomb is the receipt of victory showing that the price for sin was paid and accepted.

"And if Christ is not risen, your faith is futile; you are still in your sins!" (I Corinthians 15:17).

The blood of bulls and goats had to be offered again and again and again and again because it was a temporary covering for sin, BUT JESUS was the final lamb!!

> "...we have been sanctified through the offering of the body of Jesus Christ ONCE FOR ALL"
> (Hebrews 10:10) (emphasis mine).

HOW DO WE KNOW WHAT WE BELIEVE?

How do we know what we believe? We listen to what we say. We say what we believe. Jesus said:

> "A good man out of the good treasure of his heart brings forth good; and an evil man out of the evil treasure of his heart brings forth evil. FOR OUT OF THE ABUNDANCE OF THE HEART HIS MOUTH SPEAKS"
> (Luke 6:45) (emphasis mine).

Proverbs 23:7 tells us, "...as he thinks in his heart, so is he..." Speaking and thinking—how crucial is this? Let's look at another scripture:

> "So then faith comes by hearing, and hearing by the word of God" (Romans 10:17).

If faith comes by hearing and hearing by the Word of God, when we speak words that are full of doubt and unbelief, then faith in God is not arising. Words of faith build, fill and feed our spirit man, while words of doubt and unbelief speak to our natural man. Which do we want manifesting—our spirit or our flesh??

UNBELIEF

It wasn't murder or adultery or even idol worship that kept the children of Israel out of the promised land. It was their unbelief.

None of us card-carrying Christians would ever say we didn't believe God because, of course, we want to believe

Him all the time and in every situation. Yet, God gently spoke this to my heart:

> **"Unbelief isn't so much an overt belief that God will not; it's simply not believing that He will!!"**

Convicted!

We can believe God can do something—there is unbelief here as this gives Him an out. We can believe God will do something—that is a future belief. When we believe God IS doing something—that is the I AM who is present in every situation and in every challenge we face and is working on our behalf NOW.

WE ARE CHRISTIANS, BUT DO WE BELIEVE???

Whatever we are facing, whatever our situation, we can still believe God's wisdom is being imparted. His provision is being poured out, His direction is being given, and His deliverance is being made to manifest.

Whatever we are facing, whatever our situation, whatever the outcome, will we still believe?

The Apostle Paul was an amazing man, writing two-thirds of the New Testament. Read his "resume:"

> *"...in labors more abundant, in stripes above measure, in prisons more frequently, in deaths often. From the Jews five times I received forty stripes minus one. Three times I was beaten with rods; once I was stoned* (and this wasn't drugs!)*; three times I was shipwrecked; a night and a day I have been in the deep; in journeys often, in perils of water, in perils of robbers, in perils of my own countrymen, in perils of the Gentiles, in perils in the city, in perils in the wilderness, in perils in the sea, in perils among false brethren; in weariness and toil, in sleeplessness often, in hunger and thirst, in fastings*

> *often, in cold and nakedness—besides the other things, what comes upon me daily..."*
> (II Corinthians 11:23-28) (emphasis mine).

Yet, these were not the things he boasted of in the end. His testimony was this:

> *"I have fought the good fight, I have finished the race, I have* **KEPT THE FAITH"**
> (II Timothy 4:7) (emphasis mine).

Of all the things Paul had been through, at the end, it was keeping the faith that was so precious to him. Yes, it matters what we believe.

"WHEN" DO WE BELIEVE?

Does that seem like a weird question? This is not just a rote answer of "all the time and in every situation." Of course, we want to always believe. The question is: **When** do we believe that we have what we asked for in prayer?

Do we believe we will have the answers to our prayers when we die? Question: when do we receive an inheritance? Do we receive it when the testator dies or do we receive it when we die? Of course, we receive it when the testator dies. If we are waiting to receive health, prosperity, joy, and peace when we go to Heaven, then we've missed out on our inheritance. Those things have always been in Heaven. Jesus bought it all for us to enjoy on the earth before we ever go to Heaven.

Do we believe we receive it when we've believed enough? (Define "enough.")

We have all kinds of beliefs and most of the time we are not even cognizant of them. Let's ask the Holy Spirit to reveal the wrong beliefs, the beliefs that negate our faith, and the beliefs that stand in the way of receiving the answers:

> Holy Spirit, thank You that You came. Thank You that You are my Comforter and my Teacher, leading me into all truth. Examine my heart and expose those beliefs that are contrary to the Kingdom—righteousness, peace and joy. Illuminate Your truth to uproot unbelief so the soil of my heart is good soil, receiving faith and producing one hundredfold! Amen.

Back to the question: when do we believe? We believe when we pray, but not only that, we believe that we receive when we pray.

> *"For assuredly, I say to you, whoever says to this mountain, 'Be removed and be cast into the sea,' and does not doubt in his heart, but believes that those things he says will be done, he will have whatever he says. Therefore I say to you, whatever things you ask <u>when you pray, believe that you receive them</u>, and you will have them"*
> (Mark 11:23-24) (emphasis mine).

Read that again. When do we receive them? We receive them WHEN we pray and because we believe that we receive them, then WE WILL HAVE THEM! In connection with believing is our speaking and confessing. This scripture says we have whatever we SAY. What are we saying?

This is Jesus talking, *"For assuredly, I say to you."* He's talking to us and He's emphasizing it—"assuredly." He says we will have whatever we say (if we don't doubt in our heart).

WHAT KIND OF FAITH?

Let's look at something we are probably all familiar with—Amazon. When we order from Amazon, when do we know the order is on the way? Usually, it's initially when we place the order. If we haven't placed an order, then there is no order or request. Do we keep calling Amazon and ordering the same thing over and over and over because it hasn't shown up on our doorstep yet? No. If we do, WE DON'T BELIEVE Amazon got our order. It's like this when we pray. If we keep praying about the same thing, then WE DON'T BELIEVE God heard our prayer. If we do this, then we go from believing God and praying to not believing He heard us and we pray again. SO, we go back and forth from believing to not believing.

> *"Just make sure you ask empowered by confident faith without doubting that you will receive. For the ambivalent person believes one minute and doubts the next. Being undecided makes you become like the rough seas driven and tossed by the wind. You're up one minute and tossed down the next. When you are half-hearted and wavering it leaves you unstable. Can you really expect to receive anything from the Lord when you're in that condition?"* (James 1:6-8 TPT).

What has happened? We have gone from faith to sight. Because we can't SEE the answer, we don't believe we HAVE the answer. That is not scriptural. We live by faith, not by sight!

> *"Ask, and it will be given to you; seek, and you will find; knock, and it will be opened to you. For everyone who asks receives, and he who seeks finds, and to him who knocks it will be opened. Or what man is there among you who, if his son asks for bread, will give him a stone? Or if he asks for a fish,*

will he give him a serpent? If you then, being evil, know how to give good gifts to your children, how much more will your Father who is in heaven give good things to those who ask Him!" (Matthew 7:7-11).

Jesus points out plainly, *"ask and it will be given to you; seek and you will find; knock and it will be opened."* But just to make sure we get it, he says, *"EVERYONE who asks receives, HE who seeks finds, and to HIM who knocks it WILL BE opened."*

Jesus even points out that God is a better parent than me! *"...HOW MUCH MORE will your Father in heaven give good things to those who ask Him!"*

The Amplified says, *"ask and KEEP ON asking and it will be given to you; seek and KEEP ON seeking and you will find; knock and KEEP ON knocking and the door will be opened to you."* Instead of looking at this as a Scripture about persistence, why not look at it as a Scripture about no limit? Just because we are waiting for the answer to come to fruition, we should not limit ourselves or wait for that prayer to be answered to keep us from asking, seeking and knocking about 1,000 other things.

Is this promoting "one and done prayer?" No. James 5:16 (KJV) says:

> *"...The effectual fervent prayer of a righteous man availeth much."*

This is promoting faith in what we pray. Mark 11:23-24 says we get what we say:

> *"For assuredly, I say to you, <u>whoever says</u> to this mountain, 'Be removed and be cast into the sea,' and does not doubt in his heart, but believes that those things he says will be done, <u>he will have whatever he says</u>. Therefore I say to you, <u>whatever things you ask when you pray, believe that you receive them, and you will have them."</u>*

When we pray, we believe God has heard our prayer and then we continue to decree the answer for which we prayed. Example: "Father, bring my children back to You." I believe God heard my prayer, so every time the enemy wants me to doubt and be in fear for my children, I declare, "Father, thank You that You've heard my prayer. Thank You that Jesus died for my children and it's not Your will that any should perish. Encounter my children. You know what will get their attention. Thank You for laborers You will bring across their path. Thank You, Holy Spirit, for continually calling them. Thank You, Jesus, Your sacrifice is not in vain. Amen."

We go from asking God to declaring what we know is His will and, as Mark 11:24 says, we believe we have received what we asked for in prayer.

THE FAITH CYCLE

How do we keep believing when we do not see answers? We keep our faith activated by continuing to speak and hear in faith. Our ears hear so our heart perceives, then faith grows. What our heart perceives, our mouth speaks. What our ears hear brings faith. See the faith cycle? Hear-Faith-Speak-Hear-Faith-Speak, Hear... See the importance of speaking life, not death?

> *"Now faith brings our hopes into reality and becomes the foundation needed to acquire the things we long for. It is all the evidence required to prove what is still unseen"*
> (Hebrews 11:1 TPT).

When we have not held the answer to our prayers in our hands, we stay in faith. As defined in Hebrews, faith is the evidence or proof of things unseen. After all, once it's seen, we no longer need faith.

Do not get caught in the trap of "we need to see to believe." The truth is believing makes us see.

Don't believe that statement? How many times have we sat in traffic and our comments and thoughts are, "I can't BELIEVE this traffic!" Aren't we seeing it? Aren't we experiencing it? But we can't believe it?

What about our age? Every birthday, do we say, "I can't believe how old I am?" We've lived and experienced every day and every moment. Were we in a coma for 10 years or 10 minutes? More than likely not, but we still can't believe our age that we lived and experienced?

Neither seeing nor experiencing make us believe.

> *"For assuredly, I say to you, whoever says to this mountain, 'Be removed and be cast into the sea,' and does not doubt in his heart, but believes that those things HE SAYS will be done, he will have WHATEVER HE SAYS"*
> (Mark 11:23) (emphasis mine).

BELIEVING, NOT DOUBTING in our hearts and SPEAKING make us SEE and HAVE whatever we say.

Chapter Six

Faith

"NOW" FAITH

> *"Now faith is the substance of things hoped for, the evidence of things not seen"* (Hebrews 11:1).

My dad used to preach that the "Now" at the beginning of Hebrews 11:1 was not a conjunction, but an adjective— "now faith." When things are taking longer than hoped, when there is pain and we believe to be healed, when a financial crisis just will not break, apply "now faith." Rehearse the Word of God, which is living and powerful, and is razor sharp and discerning (Hebrews 4:12), and like a fire and a hammer that breaks the rock of impossibility and discouragement (Jeremiah 23:29). Once again, the cycle of faith begins and "now faith" arises. Hear-Faith-Speak, Hear…

Remember, God told Daniel that He had dispatched the angels to answer his prayers the first day he prayed, but the angels were warring over the demonic principalities in the heavenlies. Realize God is the generous, loving God. He is not withholding the answers.

Look at what Paul said in Ephesians 3. It is as if he could not think of enough adjectives to describe God and everything associated with God.

> *"Then you will be empowered to discover what every holy one experiences—the great magnitude of the astonishing love of Christ in all its dimensions. How deeply intimate and far-*

reaching is his love! How enduring and inclusive it is! Endless love beyond measurement that transcends our understanding— this extravagant love pours into you until you are filled to overflowing with the fullness of God! Never doubt God's mighty power to work in you and accomplish all this. He will achieve infinitely more than your greatest request, your most unbelievable dream, and exceed your wildest imagination! He will outdo them all, for his miraculous power constantly energizes you" (Ephesians 3:18-20 TPT).

In summary, Ephesians 3:18-20 says:

- We won't just discover, but we are EMPOWERED to discover!
- It's not just the love of Christ, but the GREAT MAGNITUDE of the ASTONISHING love of Christ!
- The love of Christ that is not only astonishing, but it has DIMENSIONS!
- This dimensional love is not just intimate, but DEEPLY intimate!
- This deeply intimate love isn't just close, but FAR-REACHING!
- This deeply intimate, far-reaching love is not only ENDURING, but it is INCLUSIVE!
- This enduring and inclusive love is ENDLESS, BEYOND MEASUREMENT!
- This endless, beyond measure love TRANSCENDS our understanding!
- This transcending love is EXTRAVAGANT!
- This extravagant love is poured into us, not just until we are filled, but FILLED TO OVERFLOWING!
- We are not just filled to overflowing with love, but the FULLNESS OF GOD!

- It's not our efforts, but GOD'S MIGHTY POWER working in us to accomplish this!
- HE (not us) will achieve not just more, but INFINITELY MORE!
- The infinitely more that He achieves is not just from a request, but our GREATEST request!
- Not just our dreams, but our most UNBELIEVABLE DREAM!
- Not just what we can imagine, but it EXCEEDS our WILDEST imagination!
- It's not enough to be our greatest request, unbelievable dream or our wildest imagination, but He will OUTDO IT!!!
- Will He do greater still because of HIS POWER alone? No.
- Will His MIRACULOUS Power work in us? Yes, but more.
- His miraculous power CONSTANTLY energizes us!!!

Whew! What a God! Imagine He wants to answer our prayers and bless us abundantly, but every demon in hell wants to keep us from getting the answers. We are not wrestling with God to get Him to release answers to us. We are being equipped to defeat every demon standing in our way to get what God has promised and kept for us. Jesus told us in Luke 10:19:

> *"Behold, I give you the authority to trample on serpents and scorpions, and over all the power of the enemy, and nothing shall by any means hurt you."*

HEARTS AND WORDS, WORDS AND HEARTS

This is not about the legalism of our words or the mechanics of a script. This is about believing in our hearts what God says is true. We can pay attention to our words and know what we really believe.

This is a heart issue, not just a speech issue. We can change our words, but without faith, there is no power to change our spirit man. When we believe truth and it is planted in our hearts, then we speak life words. Instead of receiving condemnation, which God never does, He convicts us of our righteousness. When something wrong is revealed in our hearts, He wants to change us.

Our words are like a thermometer—they reveal the temperature of our heart. If we think our hearts are set at 72 degrees and our mouths are speaking out 95-degree or 32-degree words, something is wrong. We need to have a heart reset. Our hearts are the thermostat and our words are the thermometer showing the actual temperature.

Years ago, I could use words to cut people up in little ribbons and figuratively leave them lying on the floor. Sadly, I was proud of that. Then the Holy Spirit convicted me. I knew my words were to be kind and loving, but my pride made me think no one could get the best of me. I asked the Holy Spirit to put a watch over my mouth. The next time I got ready to spit out the wrong words, I heard, "Stop. Don't do it!" However, I went ahead and spoke harshly. I did realize I had a second when I could have stopped. The Holy Spirit continued to tell me to stop. I gradually paid attention and now He doesn't have to stop me (most of the time) because He changed me.

The Holy Spirit doesn't want to help us keep our temper or help us hold our tongue by controlling or temporarily modifying our behavior. He wants to change us so that we no longer have these issues.

BELIEVING IDENTITY MARKERS

In the last section, some Identity Markers were given. They are SOOOO important. Even though Jesus knew who He was, Satan tried to deceive Him.

In Matthew 3, Jesus is baptized by John the Baptist. Look at the signs and wonders that accompanied this—both visual and audible:

> *"When He had been baptized, Jesus came up immediately from the water; and behold, the heavens were opened to Him, and He saw the Spirit of God descending like a dove and alighting upon Him. And suddenly a voice came from heaven, saying 'This is My beloved Son, in whom I am well pleased'"* (Matthew 3:16-17).

1) The heavens were opened.
2) The Spirit of God descended like a dove, landing on Him.
3) A voice came from Heaven.
4) That voice identified Jesus as God's BELOVED Son.
5) That voice communicated God's pleasure in Jesus.

In Matthew 4, Jesus is led by the Spirit into the wilderness. After fasting 40 days and nights, the tempter came to Jesus. What were his first words? *"If You are the Son of God..."* (vs. 3 and 5). God publicly identified Jesus with the heavens opening, the Spirit of God descending like a dove, landing on Jesus, and His audible voice being heard. Jesus had no reason to PROVE to the devil who He was. Do not get caught up in this demonic trap. Recognize these words:

"If you are a Christian…"
"If you really believed, you would…"

It's a trap. Jesus did not have to lower Himself and prove to the devil ANYTHING and neither do we.

Let us liken our Christian identity crisis to an adulthood identity crisis. What if we constantly questioned everything we did?

> ➢ "I went to my mailbox after dark! Does an adult go to the mailbox after dark?"
> ➢ "I filled up my car at 3:00 a.m. Does an adult fill up with gas at 3:00 a.m.?"
> ➢ "I had cereal for breakfast. Do adults still eat cereal?"

We are adults so we can do any of these things and it does not change our adulthood. We can't let the devil trip us up with "If you are a Christian…"

Notice, Satan did not repeat God's words. He didn't remind Jesus that God had said He was the BELOVED Son of God—the devil just questioned IF He was the Son. Satan doesn't want us to be reminded of what God has said about us.

Beware! If Satan was bold enough to come after Jesus, THE WORD, with words, after all the supernatural demonstration, he has no qualms about coming after us. We better know who we are in Christ.

WHAT IS THE BIBLE?

Although the Bible is an historical account of events from Adam forward, it is the story of Jesus. There were other storylines going on that aren't included in the Bible because they do not play into Jesus and therefore are not essential for our spiritual growth and lives. For example, Elijah was involved with a school of the prophets. If there weren't prophets prophesying to other people, then this school was a failure. Why was a school of the prophets needed if only one prophet came out every 40 years?

The Bible is God's Word speaking to US. It is a personal book. It is God telling us His plans for us, what He thinks about us and where He will take us. Remember, true humility is believing what God says about us instead of what we believe about ourselves.

By reading the stories about what God did for others, it creates faith in us to believe for God to work supernaturally in our lives. The Word of God is not just historical accounts, but examples of what God can and will do. If He's already done it, He can surely do it again.

SAME OLD, SAME OLD

Does God get bored with our prayers? He's already opened a sea, opened a river (several times), brought down a city, caused a young man to slay a giant, caused an axe head to float, caused the sun to stand still and the sun to go back, etc. Why do we pray the same prayers—heal me, prosper me, save my family? Ask God to be creative. He's already done these things. Why not ask Him to do things we've never heard about? Give Him a challenge. After all, He is God, the Creator.

Like Sarah, who had always been barren, God went against nature to bring to pass His purposes in her life. We can believe God to go against nature if it's needed to bring His purposes to pass in our lives.

Like Esther, who came to the kingdom for that time, we know we are born for our specific time and generation. Whether lying "Hamans" come against us and want to see us or our family or our generation or our country annihilated,

God can give us strategies and expose the liars, haters and murderers.

Like Caleb, who at 85, said, "Give me my mountain," we can believe God to renew our years and give us the strength and vision to see His fulfillment in our lives at any age. As Psalm 92:14 says:

> *"They shall still bear fruit in old age; They shall be fresh and flourishing,"*

PERILS OF RELIGION

Religion makes our relationship with God mechanical. Religion makes us passive, powerless and pushes us to do more works of the flesh such as:

- Read the Bible, but don't get anything out of it.
- Pray, but don't expect Him to interact.
- Pray "at" Him.
- Do our religious DUTY.

We have not been called to religious duty. This leads to rituals and there is no life in rituals!

> *"And you did not receive the 'spirit of religious duty,' leading you back into the fear of never being good enough. But you have received the 'Spirit of full acceptance,' enfolding you into the family of God…"* (Romans 8:15 TPT).

When we think we must "DO the right thing," this erroneously makes us believe we have "earned" whatever answer comes our way. Remember, the only way we receive anything from God is through faith, not works.

I was in a restaurant having lunch when I overheard an older man telling a younger man, "Read the Bible every day.

Now, you won't get anything out of it at first..." What? Where is the faith in that statement? The faith was he would not understand the Bible. That young man was now on a journey to keep his spirit and eyes closed because the Bible was too far above him. The message conveyed was, "God is not going to speak with you—just go through the motions." There are so many sad parts to this story. The young man was instructed to start his journey with God expecting nothing but dead religion. The older man told him this, not to derail him, but because it was what he believed. Both men were being robbed by a religious spirit.

We can fall into the trap of copying someone in the Bible because we want the answer they got. For example, we are in a situation where we need to be delivered like the three Hebrew children, so we stand like them. That's great, but the three Hebrew children didn't stand because it was the "right thing to do" or because they copied someone else. The three Hebrew children stood and said what they said because it was what they believed. What do we believe?? Who do we believe we are in Christ?

"Doing the right thing" is a legalistic activity. It makes us think we will receive because we did the right "work" for us to be rewarded. These are dead works.

How do you know if you are performing "works?" Listen to yourself pray. If you say, "Lord, I have done this, that and the other...," then you are expecting an answer based on your works.

We come to God based on what His word says. If He didn't mean what he said, He should not have said it. God answers our faith because faith is the currency of Heaven.

BE

God has called us to "BE."

> *"for in Him we live and move and have our BEING..."*
> (Acts 17:28) (emphasis mine).

If I "be," then I will "do." My doing comes out of WHO I am. In other words, my actions come from my heart and not my head. Doing the right thing is not actually what others or culture tells us is the right thing, but what God says and leads us to do. Remember a few years ago when WWJD (what would Jesus do) was popular? Here is what Jesus would do: whatever God told Him to do. There was no script. No formula. Did He heal the blind the same way? No. Once He spit and made clay. Another time, He healed a blind man who then saw men as trees walking. Jesus prayed again and his eyes were corrected. Did Jesus miss it? No. The Bible tells us that we are trees of righteousness (Isaiah 61:3). The man was spiritually seeing men as trees and Jesus had to dial back his vision. What Jesus would do was follow the leading of the Spirit—just like we are to do.

Identity Markers show us what God wants us to know about who we are. Remember, the heart is the thermostat and our words are the thermometer. Identity Markers are the temperature He wants our hearts to be set at!!

> *"Keep your heart with all diligence, For out of it spring the issues of life"* (Proverbs 4:23).

HOW DO WE PRAY?

We pray in faith, believing. Faith is important to God.

> *"But without faith it is impossible to please Him, for he who comes to God must believe that He is, and that He is a rewarder of those who diligently seek Him"*
> (Hebrews 11:6).

Are we confident in our prayers? God wants us to be.

> *"Now this is the confidence that we have in Him, that if we ask anything according to His will, He hears us. And if we know that He hears us, whatever we ask, we know that we have the petitions that we have asked of Him"*
> (I John 5:14-15).

AH! There's the problem. *"If we ask anything according to His will..."* Do we know what His will is? Of course, we do!

THE WILL OF GOD

Let's look at the life of Jesus. What did He do? If He did it, it must be the will of God, right?

> *"...Behold, I have come to do Your will, O God..."*
> (Hebrews 10:9).

What did Jesus do?

1) Healed people
2) Made people whole
3) Raised people from the dead
4) Multiplied food
5) Cast out demons
6) Blessed a job (Peter's boatload of fish)
7) Loved children
8) Loved the lost
9) Showed where tax money could be found
10) Calmed storms

Should I go on? Jesus said He never did anything that He hadn't seen the Father do. So, not only was Jesus doing it, but God showed Him.

The last recorded words of Jesus in Mark 16:15-16 says:

> *"...Go into all the world and preach the gospel to every creature. He who believes and is baptized will be saved; but he who does not believe will be condemned."*

That is the "Great Commission," which most Christians believe and practice fervently. However, they stop there and miss the next words of Jesus:

> *"And these signs will follow those who believe: In My name they will cast out demons; they will speak with new tongues; they will take up serpents; and if they drink anything deadly, it will by no means hurt them; they will lay hands on the sick, and they will recover"* (Mark 16:17-18).

We can't believe the first words of Jesus in Mark 16:15-16 without believing what He said in the immediately following verses.

If Jesus is telling them to do these things, shouldn't we think that it's His will for us to cast out demons, speak with new tongues, be safe with serpents (I don't believe in snake handling—remember Paul on the Isle of Malta, Acts 28), drink anything deadly without harm, and lay hands on the sick and they will recover?

Unfortunately, many times we insulate ourselves regarding God. We don't know what His will is so we don't want to get our hopes up too high. We pray, "Not my will, but thine be done," as a coverall to our prayers (maybe even a good luck charm). I'll be honest, I have prayed like this thinking God would notice my sincerity and answer because of that, but I can be "sincerely" wrong. God answers faith, not sincerity.

I heard someone say, "Faith begins where the will of God is known!" When Jesus was in the Garden of Gethsemane and said, "Not my will, but thine be done," He knew exactly what the will of God was—He had to go to the cross because it was the purpose for which He came. He couldn't get to the Garden of Gethsemane and die there. In fact, when Jesus prayed that, He was praying what He knew was NOT the will of God for Him.

Let's be honest, Jesus didn't heal everyone (skeptics will point this out), BUT He did heal everyone who came to Him. Questions: Who did Jesus ever turn down? Did Jesus ever tell anyone they couldn't be healed because God was trying to teach them something? No! He healed and delivered everyone who came to Him! II Corinthians 1:20 says:

> *"For all the promises of God in Him are Yes, and in Him AMEN, to the glory of God through us"* (emphasis mine).

Look at what Peter said about God's will:

> *"The Lord is not slack concerning His promise, as some count slackness, but is longsuffering toward us, <u>not willing</u> that any should perish but that all should come to repentance"*
> (II Peter 3:9) (emphasis mine).

Let's be geeky here a minute and look at a definition from Strong's Concordance of the Bible.[1] In this passage, "perish" is apollumi (a-paw-loo-mee) in the Greek. It means to destroy fully, (reflexively to perish or lose) literally or figuratively—destroy, die, lose, mar, or perish.

"Perish" here isn't only attributed to eternal life. Anything that destroys or causes death, or loss or mars something, is a form of perishing. Then doesn't that mean that besides death, loss is a form of perishing? Poverty is a form of perishing? Sickness is a form of perishing? Lack of vision or purpose is a form of perishing?

---

[1] James Strong, *Strong's Expanded Exhaustive Concordance of the Bible* (Nashville: Thomas Nelson, 2009).

Further, let's agree that when it says, *"not willing that any should perish, but that all should come to repentance,"* this isn't always about sin! Repentance is about a change of mind and/or direction. With that in mind, let's re-read the scripture:

> *"The Lord is not slack concerning His promise, as some count slackness, but is longsuffering toward us, <u>not willing</u> that any should perish* (suffer destruction, be destroyed, die, suffer loss or marring) *but that all should come to repentance* (a change of mind or direction)"
> (II Peter 3:9) (emphasis mine).

Would we ever say that it's God's will for anyone to die and go to hell? No, emphatically no! Then, we also don't believe it's His will for us to suffer loss, destruction, marring, or to be destroyed. Thus, we can pray for the reversal of any of those things knowing full well we are in the will of God. Remember, it's the thief who comes to still, kill and destroy! Jesus came to give LIFE, ABUNDANT LIFE! (John 10:10)

Here's another point about praying, "not my will, but thine be done." If we don't know what the will of God is, then for what are we believing? Where is our faith? Let's just take healing. If we don't know it's God's will for us to be healed and we pray, "not my will, but thine be done," which way do we believe? Do we believe in being healed or not being healed? If we don't know His will about this, then we are on the proverbial fence. We can't believe in being healed because it might not be His will. We can't believe not to be healed because He might want to raise us up. See the problem? NO FAITH IS EXERCISED!!! If God responds to faith, then to what is He going to respond?

A friend of mine pastors a church in Augusta, Georgia. Her mother was ill and she went to see her. The mother "believed" she was suffering for God, which was why she was sick. Even though she believed she was suffering for God, she was taking all kinds of medicine. My friend went to her nightstand and wiped all the medication into the wastebasket. She said, "If you are suffering for God, then suffer!"

If we believe it is God's will for us to be sick, then we should stop going to the doctor to get well or lessen our discomfort. It seems hypocritical to think we should suffer for God and then do everything we can to lessen the suffering.

I've heard Christians say their loved one was sick with a cold, but they would get better with time. Give a Scripture for that belief. Where is faith in God in that statement? If we don't exercise faith, even with a cold, we are not building our faith to use if we ever get a terminal diagnosis.

We have a cold, but we think it will just run its course. No faith needed here. We have an unexpected expense because our car breaks down. We arrange to work overtime. No faith needed here. Do we have overcoming faith or lazy faith?

Do we need Him or do we make our life as safe, comfortable and insulated as we can because we don't believe He will do anything for us? Do we believe in His finished work? What do we believe?

> Jesus died for our sins, yes? Then we believe it's God's will for us to be saved!
> Jesus was wounded for our transgression, yes? Then we believe it's God's will for our transgressions to be wiped away (Isaiah 53:5).
> Jesus was bruised for our iniquities, yes? Then we believe it's God's will for our iniquities to be stopped in their tracks (Isaiah 53:5).
> Jesus was chastised for our peace, yes? Then we believe it's God's will for us to have and be in peace (Isaiah 53:5).

- Jesus was striped for our healing, yes? Then we believe it's God's will for us to be healed (Isaiah 53:5, I Peter 2:24).
- Jesus told us to lay hands on the sick and they will recover, yes? Then we believe it's God's will for us to lay hands on the sick so they will recover (Mark 16:18).
- Jesus said cleanse the lepers, raise the dead and cast out demons, yes? Then we believe it's God's will for us to set people free and raise them up, even from death (Matthew 10:8).

Those are all great and Jesus also told us that we would do greater works, yes? Then we believe we can and will see manifestations greater than what Jesus did (John 14:12). (Wow! What would that look like?)

Would we ever believe it's God's will for us to stay in sin after Jesus paid the price for sin? NO! Then why would we believe it's God's will for us to stay sick after Jesus was striped, or poor after Jesus became poor for us to be rich, or anxious when He was chastised for our peace?

Let's get off the faith destroying "not-my-will-but-thine-be-done" fence and move in confident prayer believing for the answer we desire. Remember this about our wonderful, good, generous, loving, forgiving, trustworthy, faithful, merciful Father:

> *"...what man is there among you who, if his son asks for bread, will give him a stone? Or if he asks for a fish, will he give him a serpent? If you then, being evil, know how to give good gifts to your children, <u>how much more</u> will your Father who is in heaven give good things to those who ASK Him!"*
> (Matthew 7:9-11) (emphasis mine).

That's what we believe!

Homework:

1) One hundred times a day quote out loud:

   "Not one promise from God is empty of power. NOTHING IS IMPOSSIBLE WITH GOD!"
   (Luke 1:37 TPT) (emphasis mine).

2) Every time you are faced with an issue, new or old, quote:

   "Not one promise from God is empty of power. NOTHING IS IMPOSSIBLE WITH GOD!"
   (Luke 1:37 TPT) (emphasis mine).

3) Every time you want to dwell on an issue, new or old, stop that thought and quote:

   "Not one promise from God is empty of power. NOTHING IS IMPOSSIBLE WITH GOD!"
   (Luke 1:37 TPT) (emphasis mine).

This is not about mechanically, ritually saying it one hundred times. This is about hearing yourself say it, faith growing and then speaking it out of the abundance of your heart (the faith cycle). You will begin to believe it for every situation in your life and the lives of your friends and family. (You might be surprised how much unbelief you've had!)

This means you will say it over one hundred times. One hundred times by itself, then additional times over issues you face or issues you may want to meditate upon.

- My mortgage is due...nothing is impossible with God.
- The doctor's report is...nothing is impossible with God.
- My children aren't serving God...nothing is impossible with God.

- ➤ I lost my job. How am I going to make it?…nothing is impossible with God.
- ➤ I can't go on…nothing is impossible with God.

Section III

Purpose

Chapter Seven

What Is Our Purpose?

We can hypothesize and debate about what our purpose is all day long and for centuries, and man has. Why don't we look at the Bible to tell us what is God's purpose for man?

First of all, let's establish that the earth belongs to God:

> *"In the beginning God created the heavens and the earth"* (Genesis 1:1).

> *"The earth is the LORD's, and all its fullness, The world and those who dwell therein"* (Psalm 24:1).

> *"And he blessed him and said: 'Blessed be Abram of God Most High, Possessor of heaven and earth;"* (Genesis 14:19).

Even the days belong to the Lord:

> *"Then God said, 'Let there be light'; and there was light. And God saw the light, that it was good; and God divided the light from the darkness. God called the light Day, and the darkness He called Night. So the evening and the morning were the first day"* (Genesis 1:3-5).

> *"This is the day the LORD has made; We will rejoice and be glad in it"* (Psalm 118:24).

The seed-bearing plants and fruit bearing trees were created after their kind. The sea creatures and the birds were created after their kind. The cattle and creeping things and beasts after their kind. THEN God made man *"in Our image, according to Our likeness"* (Genesis 1:26). Adam was not just a random creation—he was created by God after God. **We are the God-kind.** We are speaking spirits. Out of all creation, we are the only God-kind. Ponder this.

What was God's direction and purpose for man?

"...let them have dominion over the fish of the sea, over the birds of the air, and over the cattle, over all the earth and over every creeping thing that creeps on the earth" (Genesis 1:26).

Did God do what He said and purposed? Look further:

"So God created man in His own image; in the image of God He created him; male and female He created them. Then God blessed them, and God said to them, 'Be fruitful and multiply; fill the earth and subdue it; have dominion over the fish of the sea, over the birds of the air, and over every living thing that moves on the earth'" (Genesis 1:27-28).

He created man. He purposed man, but BEFORE He did that, He provided for man. Everything was created before man:

"And God said, 'See, I have given you every herb that yields seed which is on the face of all the earth, and every tree whose fruit yields seed; to you it shall be for food. Also, to every beast of the earth, to every bird of the air, and to everything that creeps on the earth, in which there is life, I have given every green herb for food'; and it was so. Then God saw everything that He had made, and indeed it was very good. So the evening and the morning were the sixth day" (Genesis 1:29-31).

God blessed man and spoke to them and said:

1) Be fruitful and multiply
2) Fill the earth and SUBDUE it
3) Have dominion over the fish of the sea
4) Have dominion over the birds of the air
5) Have dominion over every living thing that moves on the earth

After the flood, God blessed Noah and his sons and said to them:

> "...*Be fruitful and multiply, and fill the earth. And the fear of you and the dread of you shall be on every beast of the earth, on every bird of the air, on all that move on the earth, and on all the fish of the sea. They are given into your hand. Every moving thing that lives shall be food for you. I have given you all things, even as the green herbs*" (Genesis 9:1-3).

God told them:

1) Be fruitful and multiply
2) Fill the earth
3) The fear/dread of you on every beast
4) The fear/dread of you on every bird of the air
5) The fear/dread of you on all that moves on the earth
6) The fear/dread of you on all the fish of the sea
7) They are given into your hand

There seems to be a theme being repeated here. David said:

> *"The heavens belong to our God; they are his alone, BUT HE HAS GIVEN US THE EARTH AND PUT US IN CHARGE"*
> (Psalms 115:16 TPT) (emphasis mine).

It appears that God wants man to have dominion of the earth. Notice this was not dominion over other people, but all of creation. God has continually corrected and guided His people toward that purpose through the centuries.

Creation is:

> *"In the beginning God created the heavens and the earth"* (Genesis 1:1).

> *"In the beginning was the Word, and the Word was with God, and the Word was God. He was in the beginning with God. All things were made through Him, and without Him nothing was made that was made. In Him was life, and the life was the light of men. And the light shines in the darkness, and the darkness did not comprehend it"* (John 1:1-5).

> *"The earth was without form, and void; and darkness was on the face of the deep. And the Spirit of God was hovering over the face of the waters. Then God said, 'Let there be light'; and there was light. And God saw the light, that it was good; and God divided the light from the darkness. God called the light Day, and the darkness He called Night. So the evening and the morning were the first day"* (Genesis 1:2-5).

THE BIG GAP

Something happened between Genesis 1:1 and Genesis 1:2. It's called the Big Gap Theory because God did not create the earth without form, void and in darkness. That's not His nature. Something happened that caused the earth to be that way.

By Genesis 2:2, God has now reset the earth. He has created everything in five days and on the sixth day, He put man in a garden on the earth—Adam in Eden. He sets out the purpose for man, including parameters: do not eat of the tree of the knowledge of GOOD and evil (not just the knowledge of evil) and the tree of life.

Imagine, God has made Adam the God-kind. All of his spirit was alive. All of his spiritual and natural senses worked. Then, the serpent deceives Eve and she shares with Adam. When God came after the fall, He couldn't find Adam. Why? God met with Adam in the spiritual and the natural realm, but now that he has fallen, his spiritual senses are dead. God can't find Adam where they normally meet. Adam has fallen from the spiritual into the natural. He has fallen from the glory. Remember, Romans 3:23:

"for all have sinned and fall short of the glory of God,"

When the parameters were set in the Garden, they were warned about eating of the tree of the knowledge of good and evil:

"but of the tree of the knowledge of good and evil you shall not eat, for in the day that you eat of it you shall surely die"
(Genesis 2:17).

And they did die that day…spiritually!

Adam and Eve originally were clothed in the glory of God (they had not yet sinned), which is why they didn't know they were naked. Now that they have fallen, their spiritual eyes are blind, but their natural eyes see their nakedness. Because of what they see, they make clothes out of leaves to cover their nakedness (an attempt to cover their spiritual nakedness, as well).

Imagine, before the fall, they met with God in the cool of the day. All their spiritual senses worked. God showed them things in the spirit because they were the God-kind. What if they could see demons outside the Garden through their spiritual senses? Now, all of their spiritual senses are dead. They know the demons are there, but they can't see them!

How does God respond to Adam's sin? He calls to Adam and says:

> "...Where are you?" (Genesis 3:9).

To which Adam replies:

> "...I heard Your voice in the garden, and I was afraid because I was naked; and I hid myself" (Genesis 3:10).

God doesn't start condemning them. He doesn't pass an oral judgment on them. He asks two simple questions:

> "...Who told you that you were naked? Have you eaten from the tree of which I commanded you that you should not eat?" (Genesis 3:11).

God asks who has caught their ear away from His voice—"*WHO told you...*"

Now was the opportunity for Adam to fess up that they had eaten from the forbidden tree, but the blame game started. If Adam would have taken responsibility and asked for forgiveness, what might God have done? Unfortunately, not only rebellion had entered, but so had FEAR.

What is God's continued response of love? He redeems them. He kills animals and covers man in the bloody skins. Hebrews 9:22 says:

> "...*without shedding of blood, there is no remission* [of sins]" (emphasis mine).

Sacrificial blood for sin wasn't just for us when Jesus gave up His life. From the first man, the shedding of blood was used to cover sin. Not only that, God put the blood covering over Eve, who was deceived, and Adam, who took freely. In other words, the blood covered ALL. In His goodness, God cast Adam and Eve out of the Garden before they could eat of the tree of life and stay eternally in that state without possible redemption. See how man already strayed and God is bringing him back into alignment?

Let's follow how God continually brought man back to His intent:

- The Flood (Genesis 6-9): Noah found grace. Man had been corrupted with demonic seed (giants), the daughters of men marrying the sons of God (fallen angels), but Noah and his family were purely human. God told Noah to build the ark. He gave him the plans. It took years to build it. God wiped out the wickedness and basically started fresh with eight humans—8 (the number of new beginnings). Eating changed as man began to eat meat. Animals are now fearful of man.
- Tower of Babel (Genesis 11): During the building of the tower, it took a year for stones to be passed from the bottom of the tower to the top. The people building the tower lived on the tower. God confused their speech so they could not fulfill their evil purpose. The tower wasn't being built to reach God, but to serve other wicked purposes. Again, God got involved to keep man on a path. He could not judge with a flood because He made covenant that He would never do that again, so He confused their speech causing man to separate.
- Abraham (Genesis 12-25): God called him out of his country. Abram looked for a city whose maker and builder was God. God restored his and Sarah's youth to bear the son of promise—Isaac. All along, God

keeps using His hand to direct man toward His purposes.

- <u>Joseph</u> (Genesis 37-50): Joseph was a descendant of Abraham. He was sold into slavery, then after being seduced without success, was lied about and thrown into prison. He was raised out of prison and made second in the land and over the provision for famine over all the known world. God's "man with the plan" directed the feeding of the nations.
- <u>Children of Israel</u> (Exodus – Joshua): The descendants of Joseph's family were enslaved for over 400 years and then delivered from Egypt. In destroying Egypt, God destroyed the systems and false gods that had been put into place. He led His people to their promised land and God told them everywhere the soles of their feet touched would be theirs.
- <u>David</u> (beginning of I Samuel 16): We know the stories of how David was anointed by Samuel as king and he defeated the uncircumcised Philistine, Goliath. God said his descendants would always sit on the throne. Jesus is a descendant of David.
- <u>Esther/Mordecai</u> (Book of Esther): The Jews were to be destroyed by the plot of Haman. Esther had become queen and faced annihilation of the Jews. God exposed Haman and he and his ten sons were hung. Mordecai was promoted to Haman's place. The laws passed by Mordecai were written in the history of the Medes and Persians, meaning the secular world was affected by Mordecai. What does that mean? Persians were the ancestors of the modern-day Iranians. Iran has Godly laws in its past!
- <u>Daniel/Three Hebrew Children</u> (Book of Daniel): We all know the story of Daniel and the three Hebrew children. The wicked wanted them destroyed—Daniel

by the lions and Shadrach, Meshach and Abednego by fire. God shut the mouths of the lions and delivered the three Hebrews in the midst of the fire. Daniel was called to interpret what the handwriting on the wall had transcribed.

> ➢ <u>Kings Had Dreams</u>: Men of God interpreted the dreams of kings and pharaohs.

There are many other stories through the Old Testament showing how God kept putting His children back in positions of authority and destroying the wickedness that wanted to thwart His plans and take over, promoting the plans of the demonic. God keeps inserting Himself into the history of man and directing it for His purposes.

As the Old Covenant is coming to an end, Jesus comes on the scene. He comes as God in the flesh. He made Himself to be poor (human) and live life as a human but filled with the Spirit of God. His death and resurrection ushered in the New Covenant that is made on better promises. Remember, the New Covenant begins with the resurrection of Jesus. He ministered under the Old Covenant through the gospels.

> *"But now He has obtained a more excellent ministry, inasmuch as He is also Mediator of a better covenant, which was established on better promises"*
> (Hebrews 8:6) (emphasis mine).

Did Jesus continue the purpose for which God created man?

- ✓ <u>Be Fruitful and Multiply</u>: Jesus had disciples. He was the Word become flesh. He gave Himself as one to be turned into untold billions. That sounds like fruitfulness and multiplication.

- ✓ <u>Dominion</u>: The storms obeyed, the fish obeyed, the demons obeyed, sickness obeyed, death obeyed, food multiplied, even the legalistic Pharisees and Sadducees were challenged and silenced by His Word. Wasn't that Jesus having dominion?

When Jesus returns, He's coming back to rule and reign. He is not coming back to deal with sin—He already did that!

> *"...The reason the Son of God was revealed was to undo and destroy the works of the devil"* (I John 3:8 TPT).

Chapter Eight

Dominion

God wants us to have dominion. Now, before we get militant and develop a "let's-take-over-the-world" attitude, let's look at this dominion.

Jesus said those who believe in His name *"will cast out demons"* (Mark 16:17). Does that sound like dominion?

In Mark 11:23, Jesus says:

> *"For assuredly, I say to you, whoever says to this mountain, 'Be removed and be cast into the sea'…he will have whatever he says."*

Doesn't that sound like dominion?

Jesus sent out the 12 disciples in Matthew 10:8 and told them, *"Heal the sick, cleanse the lepers, raise the dead, cast out demons…"* Jesus also sent out 70 in Luke 10 to do the same. Doesn't that sound like dominion?

> *"For sin shall not have dominion over you…"*
> (Romans 6:14).

Isn't it pretty clear that our Spirit man is to have dominion, not sin?

> *"And my God shall supply all your need according to His riches* (not according to our need) *in glory by Christ Jesus"* (Philippians 4:19) (emphasis mine).

Isn't that us having dominion over lack?

The enemy works overtime to get us to give up. It's easy to think:

"It's too hard."
"It's taking too long."
"My experience is no one else has seen a miracle."

We cannot live by our experience and please do not live by the theology of top 40 Christian songs. We live by faith in the Son of God who gave Himself for us and by the Word of God. God tells us what His will is. Jesus demonstrated God's will.

"…Behold, I have come to do Your will, O God…"
(Hebrews 10:9).

Did Jesus ever turn anyone away? No! Even the Syrophoenician woman in Mark 7, who came for her daughter to be delivered and had the conversation about being a dog and getting the crumbs from the master's table, got what she wanted. The delay and questioning Jesus had for her was because she presented herself as a Jew, but she wasn't a Jew. Once she admitted the truth, she got what she asked—reaching across dispensations and purposes because Jesus came for the Jews—the lost house of Israel.

Did Jesus ever tell anyone it was the will of God for them to keep their sickness or disease? No!

Did Jesus ever tell anyone God was teaching them something through their sickness or disease? No!

Did He tell the 500 who came to see Him ascend to go wait until they were good enough Jews? No!

Did He tell them to go gaze at their navels and make sure they had fulfilled the law—crossing every "t" and dotting every "i"? No! (Because He did that for us!) He told them to wait in the city of Jerusalem until they were *"endued with power from on high"* (Luke 24:49). Doesn't that sound like dominion?

Who am I? What do I believe? What is my purpose? Can you see how all of these are connected? If I don't know who I am or what I believe, I cannot know, believe or fulfill my purpose.

REIGNING IN LIFE

We can do everything Jesus did except one thing: we cannot die for anyone else's sins. We can't even earn eternal life for ourselves. Let that sink in.

Jesus said:

> *"Most assuredly, I say to you, he who believes in Me, the works that I do he will do also; and <u>greater works than these he will do</u>, because I go to My Father"*
> (John 14:12) (emphasis mine).

We are mistaken to think that Jesus did the miracles He did because He was the Son of God. If that were so, then Jesus couldn't have sent out the 12 disciples and then the 70 to perform miracles. Peter wasn't the "Son of God," but he walked on water like the Son of God.

JESUS, SON OF MAN, SON OF GOD

When Jesus was born to Joseph and Mary, He was the Son of God—He had no sin nature. Yet, He was fully human. He became poor (human—without the attributes of God) that we might be rich (full of God's spirit).

> *"For you know the grace of our Lord Jesus Christ, that though He was rich, yet for your sakes He became poor, that you through His poverty might become rich"*
> (II Corinthians 8:9).

In the natural, a baby gets its blood type from the father. Jesus had to have a heavenly father as he could not be corrupted with a fallen nature through a natural father like Joseph. If Joseph would have been his real father, then the blood of Jesus would not have been accepted as perfect to wash away sin. If Jesus would have had the blood of Joseph, He would have had a fallen nature.

Jesus was anointed by the same Holy Spirit that He anoints us with.

> *"how God anointed Jesus of Nazareth with the Holy Spirit and with power, who went about doing good and healing all who were oppressed by the devil, for God was with Him"* (Acts 10:38).

If we believe Jesus did the things He did (except suffering, dying on the cross and being resurrected) because He was the Son of God, then we won't believe we are called to do these things. If we believe we are anointed with the same Holy Spirit and power that Jesus was anointed with, then we can believe we are called to do the same things that Jesus and the disciples did. Also, because we have received the gift of righteousness, we can reign in life.

> *"For if by the one man's offense death reigned through the one, much more those who receive abundance of grace and of the <u>gift of righteousness</u> will reign in life through the One, Jesus Christ"* (Romans 5:17) (emphasis mine).

As Jesus said, we would do greater things than what He did (John 14:12), not because we are so great, but because we are filled with the same Spirit that filled and empowered Jesus.

For example, in Acts 19, handkerchiefs or aprons were brought from the body of Paul to the sick and the diseases left and the evil spirits went out of them. There is no record of Jesus doing this.

There's an old song, "To be like Jesus, To be like Jesus, All I ask, to be like Him."[2] Does that mean the only way we want to be like Jesus is suffering and dying on the cross? Hopefully, not. We are overcomers and victors because Jesus overcame and was victorious.

The Pharisees and Sadducees wanted to kill Jesus because He thought Himself equal with God. What religious spirit tries to tell us we can't be like Jesus?

> *"Therefore the Jews sought all the more to kill Him, because He not only broke the Sabbath, but also said that God was His Father, making Himself equal with God. Then Jesus answered and said to them, 'Most assuredly, I say to you, the Son can do nothing of Himself, but what He sees the Father do; for whatever He does, the Son also does in like manner. For the Father loves the Son, and shows Him all things that He Himself does; and He will show Him greater works than these, that you may marvel"* (John 5:18-20).

Isn't it interesting? Jesus told the disciples they would do greater things because God was showing Jesus greater things.

DOMINION LEADS US INTO...

Where does this dominion that God wants man to have lead us? To being liberators!! We have dominion to not only be free ourselves, but to set others free, liberating them from the effects of sin.

Where else does dominion lead us? It leads us to servanthood. Isn't that ultimately the purpose of a warrior?

---

[2] Author Unknown, *To Be Like Jesus*, accessed on November 7, 2024, at: https://hymnary.org/text/to_be_like_jesus_to_be_like_jesus_my_des.

The military exists to not only protect, take and keep ground for a king, but for the people of a nation and themselves. What a warrior does is not only for today, but for generations to come.

Imagine that we, through the power and leading of the Holy Spirit, set people free from the effects of sin. This not only affects that one person, but also their family. What if someone can't have children, but we lay hands on them and speak healing to them and then they have children? Generations will now come from the one who would have been the last.

What if the head of a household comes from generations of poverty? We, having dominion, call in the provision of the Lord. The deliverance from poverty and the manifesting provision of the Lord sets that household up for generations. Don't believe it? Didn't God set the children of Israel free from the slavery of Egypt? Didn't they leave with the goods of the Egyptians?

The dominion we have is not only for the household of faith. We set others free so they can see our God. There's nothing like manifestation as an evangelization tool.

The question needs to be asked: why does the household of faith suffer the same things as the world? Is it because it is God's will? No, it is because we have not been taught that we are to be victorious as children of the Most High God. We are waiting on Him to do it. Hasn't He already done it and provided it?

> *"Everything we could ever need for life and godliness has already been deposited in us by his divine power..."*
> (II Peter 1:3 TPT).

Somehow, we have bought into the idea that success is being prideful. It can be if we think we are so great that we have somehow "earned" the success. If we realize being a child of God means we have health, prosperity, wholeness, and wisdom, then we also must realize it's not because we are so smart, but because we have the great, loving, merciful, giving, and trustworthy God as our God.

It's not the JUDGMENT OF GOD that draws people to Him, but:

> "...the goodness of God leads you to repentance..."
> (Romans 2:4).

Let's read this story of Peter where Jesus tells him to go back to work after a profitless night of fishing:

> "...Launch out into the deep and let down your nets for a catch.' But Simon answered and said to Him, 'Master, we have toiled all night and caught nothing; nevertheless at Your word I will let down the net.' And when they had done this, they caught a great number of fish, and their net was breaking. So they signaled to their partners in the other boat to come and help them. And they came and filled both the boats, so that they began to sink. When Simon Peter saw it, he fell down at Jesus' knees, saying, 'Depart from me, for <u>I am a sinful man</u>, O Lord!'" (Luke 5:4-8) (emphasis mine).

The net-breaking, abundant, boatload of fish caused Peter to realize his sinfulness.

VICTORIOUS

Let's look at the victory Christ accomplished for us:

1) We were circumcised with the circumcision made without hands, by putting off the body of the sins of the flesh, by the circumcision of Christ.

2) We were buried with Him in baptism, in which we also were raised with Him through faith in the working of God, who raised Him from the dead.
3) We, being dead in our trespasses and the uncircumcision of our flesh, He has made alive together with Him.
4) He, having forgiven us all trespasses, having wiped out the handwriting of requirements that was against us, which was contrary to us and He has taken it out of the way, having nailed it to the cross. What was the handwriting of requirements nailed to the cross? THE LAW.
5) Having disarmed principalities and powers.
6) He made a public spectacle of them, triumphing over them in it. (Colossians 2:11-15)

"Now thanks be to God who always leads us in triumph in Christ..." (II Corinthians 2:14).

"And we know that all things work together for good to those who love God, to those who are the called according to His purpose" (Romans 8:28).

BENEFITS

Don't we love God and aren't we called according to His purpose? Then He will make all things work together for our good (another Identity Marker), even when it seems like we've been defeated and all hope is lost. He is THE redeeming, restoring God and He has benefits!!

"So I will restore to you the years that the swarming locust has eaten..." (Joel 2:25).

"Bless the LORD, O my soul, And forget not all His benefits: Who forgives all your iniquities, Who heals all your diseases, Who redeems your life from destruction, Who crowns you with lovingkindness and tender mercies, Who satisfies your mouth with good things, So that your youth is renewed like the eagle's" (Psalm 103:2-5).

Notice those are Old Testament Scriptures so they are under the Old Covenant. This is before the New Covenant, which is a better covenant with better promises. If it's a better covenant with better promises, then the good things of the Old Covenant were not taken away.

WE ARE VICTORIOUS AND HAVE DOMINION

Now, lest we think this is all a "pie in the sky" gospel, let's have a "reality" check. Paul was victorious. He had dominion, but his life was anything but roses and sunshine.

"…in labors more abundant, in stripes above measure, in prisons more frequently, in deaths often. From the Jews five times I received forty stripes minus one. Three times I was beaten with rods; once I was stoned; three times I was shipwrecked; a night and a day I have been in the deep; in journeys often, in perils of water, in perils of robbers, in perils of my own countrymen, in perils of the Gentiles, in perils in the city, in perils in the wilderness, in perils in the sea, in perils among false brethren; in weariness and toil, in sleeplessness often, in hunger and thirst, in fastings often, in cold and nakedness—besides the other things, what comes upon me daily…" (II Corinthians 11:23-28).

Yet, through all of this, Paul was victorious. For example, in the shipwreck, they all arrived alive on the shore. When he gathered firewood, a viper attached to his arm, but it did not harm him.

Isaiah 54:17 says:

> "No weapon formed against you shall prosper, And every tongue which rises against you in judgment You shall condemn. This is the heritage of the servants of the LORD, And their righteousness is from Me,' Says the LORD."

This is another dominion Scripture. Notice this does not say a weapon won't be formed against us—it just says it won't prosper. It says every tongue that rises against us, WE (not God) shall condemn. Tongues will wag. Sadly, even from other Christians.

> "Blessed be to the God and Father of our Lord Jesus Christ, who has blessed us with every spiritual blessing in the heavenly places in Christ," (Ephesians 1:3).

> "and raised us up together, and made us sit together in the heavenly places in Christ Jesus," (Ephesians 2:6).

IM (Identity Markers):

> I AM blessed in the heavenly realms with EVERY spiritual blessing in Christ.
> I AM seated with Christ in the heavenly realms.

We are blessed with every spiritual blessing in Christ. We are (already, not going to be) seated with Him. This makes us bi-dimensional. We live physically on the earth, but our spirits have Sonship and citizenship in Heaven that is already granted. We are not waiting until we die to have eternal life. We have it now. If we wait until we die, it is too late.

JESUS – OUR VICTOR

Jesus has won everything for us. He overcame everything for us so we could be victorious. IM: I AM more than a conqueror!

> *"Who could ever separate us from the endless love of God's Anointed One? Absolutely no one! For nothing in the universe has the power to diminish his love toward us. Troubles, pressures, and problems are unable to come between us and heaven's love. What about persecutions, deprivations, dangers, and death treats? No, for they are all impotent to hinder omnipotent love, even though it is written: All day long we face death threats for your sake, God. We are considered to be nothing more than sheep to be slaughtered! Yet even in the midst of all these things, we triumph over them all, for God has made us to be MORE THAN CONQUERORS, and his demonstrated love is our glorious victory over EVERYTHING!"*
> (Romans 8:35-37 TPT) (emphasis mine).

My dad used to preach that "more than a conqueror" was like a soldier's wife. The soldier went out, fought the battle, defeated the enemy, and took the spoils of war. He then gave them to his wife. She was more than a conqueror. She didn't do the work but got to enjoy the benefits. This is just what Jesus has done for us.

Jesus has given us an inheritance. Legally, we receive an inheritance when the testator (the one who leaves a Will) dies—not when we die. Jesus died, so the inheritance is for us here and now. For example, He was striped for our healing on earth—there never was sickness in Heaven. He became poor on earth because there is no poverty in Heaven. He is our peace here because there is no stress or chaos in Heaven.

I John 4:17 says, *"...as He is, so are we in this world."* Is Jesus defeated in Heaven? No, and neither are we in this world. Is Jesus sick in Heaven? No, and neither do we have to be in this world. Is Jesus poor in Heaven? No, and neither do we have to be in this world. We are not the defeated, sick and poor trying to get victory, healing and provision. We are the victorious, healed and provided for who the devil is trying to defeat, make sick and impoverished.

THE PRODIGAL

Luke 15 tells the story of the lost son. The younger son wanted his inheritance, and it says that the father *"divided to them his livelihood."* This means that the elder brother got his inheritance too.

The younger son willfully and purposely took his inheritance. He went out and lived foolishly and squandered it. Despite this, when it was all gone and after this fine, young Jewish son had fed the pigs and ate what they were eating (so low and disgusting), he decided to return home. He had no presumption to go back as a "son" but would be happy to live even as a hired servant in his father's house because it was better than the way he was currently living.

When he returned, his father saw him from a great way off and had compassion, running to the son, hugging and kissing him. The lost son admitted his sin and said he was no longer worthy to be called a son, BUT before the son could ask to be his hired servant, the father said, "Bring out not just any old robe, but the BEST robe. Put a ring (sign of authority) on his hand and sandals on his feet." The father said, "Let's have a feast. Bring the fatted calf and let's eat and be merry because my son who was 'dead' is alive and he was lost and now is found." He covered the filth of this son who had been "dead" with the robe and restored him to his place of sonship.

The elder son, who, too, had received his inheritance but had not done anything with it, maligned his lost brother by accusing him of being with harlots (was that even true?), and regaled his own righteousness.

"..these many years I have been serving you; I never transgressed your commandments at any time; and yet you

> never gave me a young goat, that I might make merry with my friends. But as soon as this son of yours came, who has devoured your livelihood with harlots, you killed the fatted calf for him.' And he (his father) said to him, 'Son, you are always with me, and all that I have is yours"
> (Luke 15:29-31) (emphasis mine).

This speaks of us. We were lost, but God washed away our sin with the blood of Jesus and gave us a ring of authority and restored us (from our fallen nature) to Sonship. The question is: are we like the elder brother who had all he could want—authority, the Father and everything the Father had—but waited to be rewarded for his works and never arose to walk in who he was?

Let's ask for the Holy Spirit to guide us:

> Holy Spirit, show us where we are squandering our Sonship and not appreciating who we are in You. In like manner, show us where we are sitting on our "righteousness" and not availing everything You have for us. Thank You for renewing our minds so that we can be transformed. Convict us of our authority and dominion stance. Amen.

KICK IT UP A NOTCH

Warrior School is not just an impartation of knowledge—what good is that? What if a person who graduates from medical school with a specialty in brain surgery decides to farm? There is nothing wrong with that, BUT the knowledge of brain surgery does nothing but sit in that person's brain. Sure, there is some knowledge that can be used in other aspects of life on the farm, but it's not saving any lives.

Haven't we been in conferences and church and revivals—hundreds of them—and received knowledge? The

Word does not tell us "the just shall live by knowledge" or "by knowledge you are saved." EVERYTHING we receive from God is by FAITH.

Warrior School is training to let us know the scriptural basis for which to believe in purpose and dominion, but knowledge alone will not change our lives in the least. God's power is not some kind of magical "poof" that happens and is not a "God is sovereign so you never know what He will do" kind of thing. If we believe that statement, then we believe God is rogue and can do anything He wants. God is not rogue. He performs His Word. We saw where Jesus never did anything the Father had not told him or shown Him beforehand. God talks more than we hear. It's our ears that aren't attuned!

He's shown us over and over in the Scriptures all the ways He can answer. That's great, but let's increase our faith. The incredible ways God has done things in the Bible and in testimonies we've heard are not the only ways God can do things. Yet, our finite minds keep praying for God to do things the same way He's done them before.

BORING PRAYERS?

Question: Is God bored with our prayers? (My question. He hasn't told me that). We pray continually for the same things, wanting the same answers that He's brought before. Yet, He has shown us He can answer in myriad ways:

- <u>Food</u> - manna on the ground or multiplying the bread and fish.
- <u>Blind eyes</u> - heal the blind eyes by touching them or spit on the ground and make mud and put on their eyes.
- <u>Lepers</u> - heal the lepers or tell them to go wash in the Jordan.

- ➢ <u>Provision</u> - multiply the oil in the cruse or cause four lepers to go to the enemy's camp and take the spoils; multiplying the bread and fish.
- ➢ <u>Water</u> - split the Red Sea or walk on water.
- ➢ <u>Creation</u> - create great fish to swallow men or have donkeys talk to their rider.

Obviously, He's not limited in ways to answer. There was only one city destroyed like Jericho. There was only one time the wind blew in the mulberry trees. There was only one time God used 300 soldiers and sent 31,700 soldiers home. There was only one time they dug ditches. There was only one David and Goliath story. God has a million ways to answer our dilemma.

RELATIONSHIP

In the earthly military, the four-star generals, colonels, captains, etc. have no relationship with the enlisted men. It is forbidden. There is a good reason for this. War requires difficult decisions. If Billy Bob is the best friend of the general, Billy Bob will probably never be put in harm's way. If that were the case, wars would never be won. Generals send men into battle knowing that some of them will not survive and even if they do, they will never be the same again. These are very hard, but necessary decisions if wars are to be won.

This is not so in God's army. He has a relationship with each and every one of us. God told Moses He was going to send an angel with him, but that wasn't enough for Moses. If God wasn't going with Him, Moses wasn't going anywhere. (Exodus 33:15)

"I'M COMING AFTER YOU, GOD!"

I am not interested in living a life of Christian theory. What is that? A life that is "supposed" to look one way, but never does. Faith that never comes to fruition. Doing the work of the Kingdom, but never seeing results. Having citizenship in Heaven, but never receiving the benefits.

This one statement has changed my entire relationship with God: "I'm coming after you, God!!" I'm not sitting waiting for God to touch me on the head like "duck, duck, goose" or to give some mandate that I, in my pride, think I can do, if I only have direction. No, I'm going after everything God has! I'm hungry for Him! It's like I can smell the Cinnabon fragrance of Him and I'm looking to see from where it's coming!! Peter saw Jesus walk on the water and his response was, 'Bid me come!' When I hear people prophesying or see saints laying hands on the sick and they recover or see testimonies of provision, I too say, "BID ME COME." I want to do that, see that, have that!

WHAT'S OUR MOTIVATION?

It's obvious we need God, but do we want Him? Do we want Him for approval and answers or do we want Him for Him?

Here are two very sad Scriptures. In Judges 16, we have the story of Delilah betraying Samson to the Philistines. Verse 20 (emphasis mine) says:

> *"And she said, 'The Philistines are upon you, Samson!' So he awoke from his sleep, and said, 'I will go out as before, at other times, and shake myself free!'* <u>*But he did not know that the LORD had departed from him.*</u>*"*

Samson did not know the Spirit of the Lord had departed from him! Let that sink in. Are we so driven, so intellectually involved, so "works" oriented that we don't recognize the Spirit of God, whether He is leading us or whether He is not? Do we know the difference between the Spirit of God being all over something and flesh being all over something? Samson HAD the anointing on him, but when the Lord had departed, he tried to accomplish in the flesh what the Lord had done before. Ouch!

This is under the Old Covenant so the Holy Spirit was not dwelling in him. Since we live under the New Covenant where the Holy Spirit is dwelling in us, are we conscious of the Lord's presence?

The second scripture is Romans 1:28 (AMP):

> *"And since they did not see fit to acknowledge God or consider Him worth knowing..."*

They did not consider God worth knowing? That's incomprehensible and sad to me. There's nothing they find curious about God to seek Him out? There's nothing they have questions about that they go directly to Him and do not trust someone else to explain Him, to represent Him, to direct them?

What about us? Are we content for others to speak for God to us or do we yearn to hear His voice, to sense His presence, to know His direction in any matter? Are we only interested in Him to know if we are being or doing right? What does He look like? Does anyone know?

THE SEVENTY-FOUR ELDERS

Let's look at a time God appeared on Mount Zion:

> *"Then Moses went up, also Aaron, Nadab, and Abihu, and seventy of the elders of Israel, and they <u>SAW</u> the God of Israel. And there was under His feet as it were a paved work of sapphire stone, and it was like the very heavens in its clarity. But on the nobles of the children of Israel He did not lay His hand. So they <u>SAW</u> God, and they ate and drank"*
> (Exodus 24:9-11) (emphasis mine).

Seventy-four people (probably 75 because Joshua was always around) SAW God. They ate and drank with God. We would think no one would ever doubt God after that! Yet, the children of Israel were content to let Moses hear from God. They were happy to stay at the bottom of the mountain. Moses knew the ways of God while the children of Israel only knew His acts.

From the encounter with the elders, God called Moses and he took Joshua to go up the mountain where God gave Moses the ten commandments. God wrote in stone! How awesome—it had never been done before!

What happened to Aaron, Nadab, and Abihu, and the seventy elders who saw God? While Moses and Joshua went up the mountain, the others went down the mountain back to the camp. Moses was 40 days on the mountain and within those 40 days, Aaron and the 70 elders built a golden calf!!!! These were the men who SAW God!

Do not be deceived to think that one great encounter with God will make us always believe Him. An encounter, even with God, can turn into a memory. Every day, every situation gives us the opportunity to believe, trust and love Him (or not).

BELTESHAZZAR

In the Book of Daniel, we have another story. Belteshazzar was eating and drinking in the palace when a hand wrote on the wall giving the pronouncement that he had been weighed in the balances and he had been found wanting. In other words, he was not weighty enough in character to tip the scale in his favor. He was assassinated that night. We are talking crazy stories of the supernatural, miraculous demonstration of the power of God!

In I Corinthians 4:20, Paul said:

"For the kingdom of God is not in word but in power."

1) Why has the 20th-21st Century church settled for sitting on the pews and being preached at and not demonstrating the manifestation of the kingdom??? Getting saved is important, but it's not all there is. It's the launching point.
2) Why do churches have lists of prayer requests for sick people a mile long, but NEVER preach a sermon on healing or lay hands on the sick? How does faith come? By hearing! Why has some of the church accepted the lie "healing is not for today?"
3) Why are Christians as broke as those who don't serve God? Many believe "poverty is next to godliness," but that is not scriptural.
4) See how unbelief and the doctrines of demons have become accepted and believed. Wouldn't the devil want the church—God's people on the earth—to believe that God isn't moving today? Wouldn't he be happy if we were obsessed with keeping the law—gazing into our navels to see if we had done everything right not believing that Jesus fulfilled the law for us? Wouldn't he be happy if we were all impoverished, dead or destroyed? Remember what Jesus said in John 10:10:

"The thief does not come except to steal, and to kill and to destroy..."

Warrior School is not for informational purposes. It's an equipping for us to manifest the Kingdom of God in our life, our family, our property, and our sphere of influence! See the picture? Along with us, another manifests the Kingdom of God in their life, their family, their property, and their sphere of influence, and then the circles begin to converge. Then the next faith filled, overcoming Christian manifests dominion in their circle…then the next faith filled, overcoming Christian manifests dominion in their circle. We can see how this could become exponential and explode. Receive revelation to see things and hear things that causes faith to arise like a geyser. Once we've seen it and heard it (revelation), we won't ever be able to unsee or unhear it.

In the latter part of John 10:10 (TPT) (emphasis mine), Jesus says:

> "…*But I have come to give you <u>everything</u> in abundance, <u>more than you expect</u>—life in its fullness until you overflow!*"

OPENED EYES

After Jesus had risen from the dead, there was a couple who walked on the road to Emmaus. Jesus walked along with them, but they didn't recognize Him. They talked. He asked them questions. Look at this exchange:

> "…*Are You the only stranger in Jerusalem, and have You not known the things which happened there in these days?' And He said to them, 'What things?' So they said to Him, 'The things concerning Jesus of Nazareth, who was a Prophet mighty in deed and word before God and all the people* (they didn't believe He was the Son of God, just a prophet),…*But we were hoping* (past tense) *that it was He who was going to redeem Israel…*" (Luke 24:18-19,21) (emphasis mine).

Jesus then explains to them:

> "*And beginning at Moses and all the Prophets, He expounded to them in all the Scriptures the things concerning Himself*" (Luke 24:27).

They got NOTHING from being with Jesus, even from His explanation. (Have you ever been like that?) They asked Him to stay with them. They took bread, blessed it and broke it, THEN THEIR EYES WERE OPENED. Jesus walked with them. Jesus, THE Son of God, THE Word become flesh, expounded from the Scriptures who He was. What did they get? Their hearts burned within them, BUT THEY STILL DIDN'T SEE JESUS. We cannot stop short of seeing Him with whatever manifestations happen (burning hearts, goosebumps). Jesus did not send the Holy Spirit to fill us with power just for us to get a few goosebumps now and then, or even every time we are with Him. The question is how much does an encounter with Jesus change our lives and overflow to work in the lives and situations of others, as well?

TSK, TSK, TSK

I used to talk about situations. My righteous indignation might burn. Maybe my smug self-righteous, religious self would feel elevated because I had the answer and just knew if they "did the right thing" or "stopped" what they were doing, their situation would change. I was thinking, "Tsk, tsk, tsk!" I felt good about myself. Superior. I knew SO MUCH! Then one day, my lightning-fast mind realized all my "tsking" wasn't doing one thing. It was only entertaining a religious spirit and leaving people stuck in their situations. Now, when I hear of situations, I send the Word to heal them. I set them free from oppression. I ask God to encounter them. I take action in the Spirit (and in the flesh, if possible).

OPINIONS HAVE TO GO

Our opinions have to go. Why? Because we set them in stone. We will believe we are correct because of our "opinion." It's a luxury we cannot afford. Why? They harden our hearts and make it harder to hear the Lord's voice of compassion. Opinions make us think people have gotten what they deserve (law). Yet, Jesus tells us to "roll away the stone!" "Take off their grave clothes!" This will be discussed in the next section.

> *"So search your hearts every day, my brothers and sisters, and make sure that none of you has evil or unbelief hiding within you. For it will lead you astray, and make you unresponsive to the living God"* (Hebrews 3:12 TPT).

Opinions and unbelief make us unresponsive to the living God!! Didn't God tell the children of Israel to take the promised land? God spoke. Didn't their unbelief and opinion make them balk and desire to go back to Egypt and keep an entire generation from their promise from God?

GET OFF THE FENCE

When we pray, do we think there's a 100% chance for God to answer our prayer or is it only a 50/50 chance? 50% chance He will answer. 50% chance He won't answer. What do you believe? 50/50 is not scriptural. If we are there, then we've begun to believe in experiences, not the Word of God. Straddling a fence is not standing in faith. Get off the fence and stand!

ANGELS ON HIGHWAYS

A few years ago, we heard of weekly accidents on I-485, which is the beltway around Charlotte, where I live. People were drunk and driving the wrong way on the highway hurting or killing other people and/or themselves. Why was that happening on our watch? We commanded the angels to be placed at the entrance ramps to I-485, not allowing any people who were going in the wrong direction to get on the highway. We never heard another story about it happening again. The power and authority of God working in us benefits not only us, but all the other people driving the highway! God loves all people!

Again, we heard of accidents on the north side of Charlotte on I-85. My mom and I got in the car one day and drove around the beltway. We used our authority and commanded the angels to protect the highways and byways. While driving on this stretch of highway, we were between two tractor trailers when one started coming over in our lane. Wielding our authority, no harm came to us, and we stopped hearing of those accidents. We weren't being affected, but others were, and the authority of the Kingdom brought protection.

TEETH ON THE BOTTOM

My great grandfather was an oysterman on Chesapeake Bay in Maryland back in the late 1920s. One day, he was out on the boat and his dentures fell into 17 feet of water. He went home and prayed. He told God it was the Depression and he didn't have money for new dentures, so he needed to find those lost teeth. The next day, he went back out on the water with two other men who had come along just to see what was going to happen. Now, with tides and water and something as light as dentures, they would not be in the same spot as where they fell into the water—there was no exact marking. Who wants to put dentures back in their mouth after they have been on the bottom of the bay with everything else?!! This did not cause my great grandfather to hesitate.

As the boat went out, he prayed in the Holy Ghost until he heard the Lord say, "Stop." He then told the men to stop the boat. He put his 20-foot oyster tongs down and pulled up the teeth on the very first try. The men jumped out of the boat and swam back to shore. When asked why they jumped out, they said there was too much God in the boat.

Because of this story from our great granddad, two of my cousins believed to find a watch that had fallen in the water and then the other believed to find his wedding ring that had fallen into a rushing, mountain stream! And they both did. They knew they served the same God.

PROTECTION FOR STUDENTS

One Saturday, God had a group I was leading go on a field trip. We drove to a community college—representing all colleges. We drove to an academy—representing all academies. We went to primary, elementary, middle, and high schools—representing all schools. We placed angels on assignments. We called forth revival. We called forth truth and pulled down the wicked. We commanded teachers who were indoctrinating students to leave their "jobs" and called people forth to train and teach children. We put angelic protection on these campuses and commanded safety for all children. We declared if anyone was coming on a campus for any nefarious reason, they would be turned around.

The very next week, a gunman went on a high school campus and killed a teacher and a student. Then he was killed by police. It was reported he had 600 rounds of ammunition. We were very sorry for the three lives lost, but it could have been a massacre. We believe God answered our prayers and saved many people that day. We believe He will continue to answer our prayers.

You, too, have authority and dominion. Your assignment is to use it.

Need provision? Here's an example of a prayer: "God, the Word says in Philippians 4:19, You shall supply all my needs, according to Your riches in glory, not according to my need. I believe You. How do You want to fulfill that?"

Is the devil harassing you? Stop listening to him. Tell him to hush (either he's talking or you're declaring!) and you start speaking to him: "I AM the righteousness of God in Christ. I resist you. Now, FLEE!!! God, how do You want him defeated today?"

Isn't God in control? Yes, THROUGH US!!! **He allows what we allow!** Ponder that!

Assignment:

Record below where or when you have recently used your authority and the victory that resulted. Be sure to date it! This gives you a record on which to look back and be encouraged.

_____

_____

_____

_____

_____

_____

_____

_____

_____

_____

_____

_____

_____

_____

_____

_____

_____

_____

_____

_____

SECTION IV

LIBERATION

Chapter Nine

Liberated Liberators

ARE WE BUT MERE MEN?

> *"...For where there are envy, strife, and divisions among you, are you not carnal and behaving LIKE MERE MEN?"*
> (I Corinthians 3:3) (emphasis mine).

No, we are not mere men. If we know Jesus, we are humans who have been made a new creation.

> *"Therefore, if anyone is in Christ, he is a new creation; old things have passed away; behold, all things have become new"*
> (II Corinthians 5:17).

Aren't we the Kingdom of God walking forth?
One of the last things Jesus said before He ascended was:

> *"And these signs will follow those who believe: In My name they will cast out demons; they will speak with new tongues; they will take up serpents; and if they drink anything deadly, it will by no means hurt them; they will lay hands on the sick, and they will recover"* (Mark 16:17-18).

- ✓ Feeding the poor is good—people without God can do that.
- ✓ Hospital visitation is good—people without God can do that.
- ✓ Holding people's hands while they die is good—people without God can do that.

- ✓ Laying hands on the sick causing them to recover—only people with God can do that.
- ✓ Casting out demons—only people with God can do that.
- ✓ Raising people from the dead and holding their hand while doing it—only people with God can do that.
- ✓ Living in divine health—only people with God can do that.
- ✓ Living with true prosperity—spiritual and physical—only people with God can do that.

Jesus became like us so we could be like Him. Acts 10:38 tells us He was anointed by the same Holy Spirit that anoints us.

Paul said:

"For the kingdom of God is not in word but in power"
(I Corinthians 4:20).

The world needs the church walking in the power and demonstration of the Kingdom. So, how do we do that? We walk in the Spirit!

SPIRITUAL SENSES

Just like our physical man, our spiritual man has five senses—sight, taste, touch, hearing, and smelling. These have to be working or we miss out on what God is doing.

Wouldn't we pray for healing if we were blind or couldn't taste or couldn't hear or smell in the natural? How disastrous would it be if we had no sensitivity to touch? If we didn't feel, we wouldn't remove our hand from a fire. Our spirit man should be functioning too.

Do we expect to hear, see, feel, smell, and taste the things of the Spirit? We should. Our spirit man is ALIVE.

When Jesus taught, He said over and over, *"he who has ears to hear, let him hear."* He wasn't talking about the flaps on the side of our heads to hear His words. He was talking about spiritual ears. If our spiritual ears aren't open, then we can't perceive things of the Spirit. If we are spiritually deaf, how can we hear God speak? In the natural, our hearing is the last to shut down. People who have come back from comas have said they heard everything said while they were comatose. While hearing is the last to go in the natural, I believe it's the first to come in the Spirit.

If we can't hear the Spirit of God calling us with the gospel, then how can faith arise for us to be saved? The Bible says that God has given to every man the measure of faith. What is that measure? It's the measure of faith needed to get saved. After that, we can grow it and grow it.

"Lovers of God have been given eyes to see and ears to hear from God" (Proverbs 20:12 TPT).

Dreams and visions are seeing in the Spirit. This sight is not only for "chosen" people. Seeing in the Spirit is not only natural, but very necessary. If we don't think spiritual senses are important, then we won't believe and expect our senses to be activated.

"The prophecy of Isaiah describes them perfectly: Although they listen carefully to everything I speak, they don't understand a thing I say. They look and pretend to see, but the eyes of their hearts are closed" (Matthew 13:14 TPT).

Jesus spoke in parables—not for people to understand, but so they would not understand. It was for them to spiritually perceive. Jesus privately explained the parables to the disciples. He explained:

> *"...it has been given to you to know the mysteries of the kingdom of heaven, but to them it has not been given. For whoever has, to him more will be given, and he will have abundance; but whoever does not have, even what he has will be taken away from him. Therefore I speak to them in parables, because seeing they do not see, and hearing they do not hear, nor do they understand"* (Matthew 13:11-13).

See the importance of perceiving with our spirit? What about taste? Is there spiritual taste? Yes, there is.

> *"especially now that you have had a taste of the goodness of YAHWEH and have experienced his kindness"*
> (I Peter 2:3 TPT).

> *"Oh, taste and see that the L*ORD *is good…"* (Psalm 34:8).

Is there spiritual smell? Yes, imagine we spiritually smell like Cinnabon. It draws people to hear the gospel.

> *"…through us diffuses the fragrance of His knowledge in every place. For we are to God the fragrance of Christ among those who are being saved and among those who are perishing"*
> (II Corinthians 2:14-15).

Once we are saved, it's only "natural" to be supernatural! It's not natural for us not to be supernatural. If we are unaware of the supernatural, we can ask God to activate our spiritual senses. God wants us, as His children, to be whole—naturally and spiritually.

> *"…he who loves Me will be loved by My Father, and I will love him and MANIFEST Myself to him"*
> (John 14:21) (emphasis mine).

SPENDING TIME WITH JESUS

Have you ever seen Jesus? I have several times. One day, He asked me to spend the day with Him. How could I refuse? I will be honest. I questioned whether I was really hearing from Jesus. I wasn't feeling 100% so I took a sick day. Jesus came and asked me to go "tubing" with Him. He had big, bright yellow innertubes for us to go tubing down a river. I said, "Yes."

All day long, I would look back at Him and He had the biggest smile on His face. He was having fun too, but He was overjoyed that He was with me and that I was having fun. His smile was magnetic. I knew He absolutely loved me. Because I could see and feel His acceptance of me, it broke down any fears or walls of my own insufficiencies and it made me love Him more deeply. I have heard other people who have seen Him talk about His smile and it immediately brings back this memory. This was a vision or an encounter as I was not actually in or near the water.

I had another encounter with Jesus. I was taking an online prophetic course. Many times, people with the gift of seeing will ask others to look for Jesus in the room. That was what the instructor asked the students to do. At the time, I had sold my house and was living with one of my daughters while I looked for my next house. I was in my bedroom and I looked around and sensed Jesus was in the far-left corner. I was sitting in a chair and my bed was in between us. Jesus came to me—not around the bed, not over the bed, but THROUGH the bed. He handed me a white, shiny stone.

Weird? Not at all, really.

"He who has an ear, let him hear what the Spirit says to the churches. To him who overcomes I will give some of the hidden manna to eat. And I will give him a white stone, and on the

stone a new name written which no one knows except him who receives it" (Revelation 2:17).

ANOTHER IDENTITY MARKER

In June of 2021, the Lord told me that I was a Liberator. I asked Him for a Scripture to back it up, so He immediately did:

> "*The Spirit of the LORD is upon Me, Because He has anointed Me To preach the gospel to the poor; He has sent Me to heal the brokenhearted, To proclaim <u>liberty</u> to the captives And recovery of sight to the blind, To set at <u>liberty</u> those who are oppressed; To proclaim the acceptable year of the LORD"* (Luke 4:18-19) (emphasis mine).

Notice, "liberty" is mentioned twice. When we give someone liberty in a situation, we have liberated them. Therefore, we are a liberator. This was the Scripture Jesus read in the synagogue. It just "happened" to be the portion of Scripture being read the day He just "happened" to be asked to read. He read about Himself. Imagine hearing Jesus, the Word become flesh, reading about Himself. Yet, they did not perceive who He was.

One of my IMs: I AM a liberator.

Isaiah 61 goes on to say:

> "*The Spirit of the Lord GOD is upon Me…To comfort all who mourn, To console those who mourn in Zion, To give them beauty for ashes, The oil of joy for mourning, The garment of praise for the spirit of heaviness; That they may be called trees of righteousness, The planting of the LORD, that He may be glorified"* (Isaiah 61:1-3).

This is the goodness and nature of our wonderful Father.

Let's be nerdy again. "Liberate" in the dictionary means:

lib·er·ate (lĭb'ə-rāt')
tr.v. lib·er·at·ed, lib·er·at·ing, lib·er·ates 1. To set free, as from oppression, confinement, or foreign control. [Latin līberāre, līberāt-, from līber, free; see leudh- in Indo-European roots.][3]

The whole scripture in Luke 4 and Isaiah 61 talks about liberation!

1) Preach the gospel to the poor (power of God unto salvation): liberation from poverty (spiritual, physical, mental, and financial)
2) Heal the broken-hearted: liberation from grief
3) Proclaim liberty to captives: liberation from captivity (strongholds)
4) Recovery of sight to the blind: liberation from blindness
5) Liberty to the oppressed: liberation from slavery and oppression
6) Proclaim the acceptable year of the Lord: liberation from hopelessness

Freedom! Imagine that. God wants people free from sin and any kind of oppression and captivity. Yet, how can we minister this freedom if we are bound ourselves?

From the enemy's perspective, the best kind of captivity is the kind where the captive doesn't know he's captive or believes that he's captive because he's "less than" the captor. (Remember, the children of Israel were enslaved by the

---

[3] American Heritage® Dictionary of the English Language, Fifth Edition. Copyright © 2016 by Houghton Mifflin Harcourt Publishing Company. Published by Houghton Mifflin Harcourt Publishing Company. All rights reserved.

Egyptians—a nation lesser in number than themselves.) Clever, huh? Once the captive adopts and accepts this mindset, keeping the captive in captivity takes little effort. Any time a captive tries to escape, the captor just causes a little hardship or pain, and they will usually get right back in line—in captivity!

What are captive mindsets in captivity?

> "What's the use?"
> "It doesn't matter what I do…"
> "This is my lot in life."
> "When life hands you lemons, make lemonade."

We are not talking about unsaved people here. If it were just the unsaved, it would be understandable. Unsaved people are without hope and under the dominion of sin. This is totally unacceptable for Christians.

Christians should not be as broke, hopeless, sick, lonely, and visionless as people without the advantage of the Holy Spirit and spiritual senses that are alive.

Chapter Ten

Lazarus

Let's look at some wonderful truths in John 11 about Lazarus. Truth is important because it sets us free.

Lazarus has died. He's been dead four days! There was a belief the Jews held that a person's spirit would hang around them for three days. In other words, in their view, there was absolutely no hope for Lazarus. The other people Jesus had raised from the dead had not been dead this long. The Jews buried the dead before sunset of the day they died. The widow of Nain's son was raised in his funeral procession. Therefore, he had only died that day. The daughter of Jairus, one of the leaders of the synagogue, died while Jesus was on the way to heal her. Lazarus was someone who was dead longer than anyone else Jesus had raised.

This is beyond the "when" belief of Mary and Martha. (Remember, in Section 2: "When" do we believe?") They believed Lazarus could have been kept from dying if Jesus had been there. Now that he's dead, they don't believe. They believed that Lazarus would be raised in the resurrection at the last day, but not today. Even others around asked if Jesus couldn't have kept this man from dying. Their belief was in the keeping, not the raising from the dead. What they didn't know yet was that He could do both. He didn't just have keeping power. What was the Identity Marker for Jesus here? One of my IMs: "**I AM** the resurrection and the life!"

Let's continue:

> *"Jesus wept. Then the Jews said, 'See how He loved him!' And some of them said, 'Could not this Man, who opened the eyes of the blind, also have kept this man from dying?' Then Jesus, again groaning in Himself, came to the tomb. It was a cave, and a stone lay against it. Jesus said, 'Take away the stone.' Martha, the sister of him who was dead, said to Him, 'Lord, by this time there is a stench, for he has been dead four days.' Jesus said to her, 'Did I not say to you that if you would believe you would see the glory of God?' Then they took away the stone from the place where the dead man was lying. And Jesus lifted up His eyes and said, 'Father, I thank You that You have heard Me. And I know that You always hear Me, but because of the people who are standing by I said this, that they may believe that You sent Me.' Now when He had said these things, He cried with a loud voice, 'Lazarus, come forth!' And he who had died came out bound hand and foot with graveclothes, and his face was wrapped with a cloth. Jesus said to them, 'Loose him, and let him go'"*
> (John 11:36-44).

Let's break this down.

JESUS WEPT

> *"Jesus wept. Then the Jews said, 'See how He loved him!' And some of them said, 'Could not this Man, who opened the eyes of the blind, also have kept this man from dying?' Then Jesus, again groaning in Himself, came to the tomb…"*
> (John 11:35-38).

Let's make Jesus real. Jesus didn't weep because He was sad. He was getting ready to raise Lazarus from the dead. Why would He cry because he was dead? Look further. Jesus wept and then He groaned to Himself. Imagine Jesus thinking, "God, how much do I have to do for these people before they believe? Even Martha and Mary, who have been with Me so long and have seen all the other things I have done, lost hope! Even when I tried to lead them into believing for resurrection, they couldn't believe it was for today."

TAKE AWAY THE STONE

> *"...It was a cave, and a stone lay against it. Jesus said, 'Take away the stone.' Martha, the sister of him who was dead, said to Him, 'Lord, by this time there is a stench, for he has been dead four days.' Jesus said to her, 'Did I not say to you that if you would believe you would see the glory of God?' Then they took away the stone from the place where the dead man was lying..."* (John 11:38-41).

Jesus said, "Take away the stone." Uncover the thing that is rotting, stinking and dead. Martha could not stand the hope. More than likely, she and her sister hoped and hoped Jesus would get there to heal Lazarus before the worst thing they could imagine happened. She couldn't bear to raise her hopes again. She couldn't accept false hope. Nevertheless, they obeyed (obedience, but no belief).

BELIEVE THAT YOU SENT ME

> *"...And Jesus lifted up His eyes and said, 'Father, I thank You that You have heard Me. And I know that You always hear Me, but because of the people who are standing by I said this, that they may believe that You sent Me"*
> (John 11:41-42).

Don't you love the confidence of Jesus? He says He knew that God always heard Him. Why did He want God to do it? Did He want God to raise Lazarus because they would be more eager to be obedient? NO! He wanted them to BELIEVE that He was sent by the Father.

Obedience is important, but let's look at the following.

Strong's Concordance of the Bible says the word "obey" is found in the Old Testament 85 times and only 34 times in the New Testament. The word "believe" is found only 45 times in the Old Testament, but 272 times in the New Testament. It's found 138 times in the gospels and 99 times in the Book of John alone.

In the Old Testament under the Old Covenant, obedience was key, but obedience doesn't necessarily make us believe. In the New Testament or New Covenant, Jesus taught us over and over to "believe" in our hearts. There was a change from the Old to the New Covenant.

Obedience doesn't lead to believing but believing will lead to obedience. For example, a soldier will obey his commanding officer. That's what a soldier does. He goes into conflict often putting his own life in danger. Does he BELIEVE in his mission? Maybe not, but he's going to obey. His obedience doesn't necessarily make him believe. Because we believe our God, we will obey Him.

COME FORTH

> *"Now when He had said these things, He cried with a loud voice, 'Lazarus, come forth!' And he who had died came out bound hand and foot with graveclothes, and his face was wrapped with a cloth. Jesus said to them, 'Loose him, and let him go'"* (John 11:43-44).

Jesus called forth "Lazarus" because if He would have just said, "Come forth," anyone who was dead would have come out of their graves. Lazarus was alive, but he was still bound hand and foot with graveclothes and his face was wrapped with a cloth. He could have jumped home behind Martha and

Mary—he's alive. Yet, he wouldn't have been able to go anywhere with them—his hands and feet were bound. He wouldn't have been able to converse with them—his face was wrapped with a cloth. He would have been like a mummy. Grave clothes affect where we go (bound feet), what we do (bound hands), what we see, and what we say (face wrap). Lazarus would have eventually died again because he couldn't eat. The second death would have been worse than the first. What good is someone brought to life who is still trapped in death clothing? Selah! (Stop and think on this.)

LOOSE AND LET GO

When people are saved—brought to spiritual life—do we continue to set them free by taking away their grave clothes? Do we see the things that held them spiritually dead taken away so they can now be spiritually alive? We don't want to leave anyone in their grave clothes. Yes, they have been made a new creation, but there are so many traumas the enemy has perpetrated in their lives, even from when they were a child. The enemy doesn't care if we get saved. If we continue to be sick and traumatized, he manipulates us like a puppet.

Set them free!!!

LIBERATORS – GO TO WORK

Here is where we partner with Jesus. Jesus told them to roll away the stone. We all have had things in our lives that have died. We put a stone over the top with the understanding it is not to be touched. Not only is there a stone, but we build an emotional fence around it 10 feet thick. It's dead. It's beyond hope. It stinks. It's rotting or already rotted. (I speak as one with experience!)

We can roll away the stone—there is HOPE! We can tell people, "You don't have to be in your sins anymore! You don't have to mourn anymore! You don't have to be poor anymore! You don't have to be sick anymore! You don't have to be tormented any longer! You don't have to carry the emotional pain anymore! You can take down the 10-foot-thick fence that was meant to keep others out, but only imprisoned you!!!" This is what we can do. Liberators, take away the stone!

Jesus is the one who gives life. *"Lazarus, come forth."* He calls them out of darkness into His marvelous light.

> *"...I have come that they may have life, and that they may have it more abundantly"* (John 10:10).

Jesus doesn't just bring life, but MORE ABUNDANT LIFE!

LIBERATE THE LIBERATORS

How many people go for counseling, whether to a pastor, psychiatrist or psychologist, for things that happened as adults? Not many. Most deal with adult issues because of things that happened to them as children.

Satan comes to children when they do not have filters in place or are not equipped to deal with situations mentally, spiritually or emotionally. He continues his attacks when we are adults too. This causes trauma and brokenness. Through this, he gains entrance to bring effects of this brokenness into our lives (he does not possess us—he demonizes us).

When a parent has allowed spirits to work in their lives, it opens their children to these spirits because the spirits have now become familiar spirits. The parents and children are not even aware these spirits should not be working in their lives. To them, it's just normal. A spirit of fear may have been camouflaged as "worry" or "concern," which becomes controlling and dictatorial. When we live with something, we "assume" everyone else lives the same way.

Whatever we excuse, we allow. The "reason" is what opens the door. What does that mean? Let's say we are depressed because we are poor. We opened the door because of our poverty. Then, our circumstances change and we are no longer poor, but because the spirit of depression was allowed to come in when there was a "reason" or an "excuse," it now has permission to stay even though the reason has changed.

PERSONAL STORIES OF FREEDOM

I have a personal story regarding this. When I was younger, I suffered from depression. Not all the time, but it was just a pall that hung over my life. One Sunday, my dad preached on Romans 6:16:

> *"Do you not know that to whom you present yourselves slaves to obey, you are that one's slaves whom you obey, whether of sin leading to death, or of obedience leading to righteousness?"*

Revelation hit me like a ton of bricks. I realized I was presenting myself as a slave to obey depression. It would tell me I needed to go home and cry. Of course, the accusation said no one would want to be with me because I was so miserable. I could control my crying until I got home so obviously (or not so obviously) I had control over it. I was serving depression. I had made it a "god" and obeyed it—feeling bad when it told me to feel bad, crying when it told me to cry. I decided right then and there I was not serving that "god" anymore. There is only one God and it's the living, loving, freeing, almighty God!

Well, I didn't have long to wait and see which god I was going to serve. The very next day, depression tried to come on me. I felt the same urge to go home, be alone and cry. Instead, I decided to go to the mall. This was huge because I didn't want to go to the mall when I felt good, much less depressed. I went and sat on a bench and watched the people going by. I refused to let the spirit have dominion over me. After a while, I left feeling happy and victorious.

Don't be deceived, that spirit still tries to exercise dominion occasionally, but it's not my god. I don't serve it.

Let me address a spirit of rejection. I am familiar with this spirit too. Through many circumstances, this spirit interjected itself into my family. There were plenty of "reasons" for this spirit to be there, but a reason can be an invitation for a spirit to stay. If we open the door, then when the "reason" changes, the spirit doesn't want to leave his home.

To deal with the spirit of rejection, I allowed pride to come in because my thought was "Bless God, no one is going to treat me that way!" Now, I have not only opened the door to a spirit of pride but have just set myself up to fall because Proverbs 16:18 says, *"Pride goes before destruction, And a haughty spirit before a fall."* Then a spirit of fear comes in because I'm afraid I will be rejected again. See the demonic party going on?

Once we have inadvertently given a spirit permission to torment us, it constantly reinforces itself. For example, a spirit of rejection might work like this: we hear about a party, but we weren't invited. In our thinking, we were obviously rejected. We call or text someone and they don't return the communication—again, REJECTION. We speak to someone and they roll their eyes—REJECTED (we didn't know they had a Bluetooth device in their ear and were reacting to the person on the phone). Through a series of events, we begin to accept "rejection" as our lot in life and it's the "truth" by which we live and the roadmap we follow.

We can see why abused people abuse people and hurt people hurt people. These are familiar spirits at work. When an abused person abuses and hurts someone else, the door has been opened for that spirit to come against that person. Abused people are afraid of people finding out they've been abused. Why do abused people carry shame, guilt and fear when they were only a victim? Because it's the demonic at work. Trauma opens the door for spirits and **spirits never come alone**. Remember what I said above about rejection, then pride and fear came along? See (spiritually perceive) the cycle—trauma, pride, fear… remembrance of the trauma, pride, fear…

SPIRIT OF FEAR

The spirit of fear almost always accompanies every other spirit. It is ancient. It was present in the Garden after Adam and Eve fell and they hid themselves from God. The Word is clear that fear is a spirit and it is not from God.

> *"For God has not given us a spirit of fear, but of power and of love and of a sound mind"* (II Timothy 1:7).

> *"…perfect love casts out fear, because fear involves torment…"* (I John 4:18).

Neville Johnson was a minister from New Zealand. There was a season of about three months in his life when God opened his eyes to see in the spirit realm. It almost drove him crazy! He said it is unnecessary to wonder if Satan can read our minds. He said spirits give off colors so he can look at us and tell what or if anything is tormenting us. In this season of his seeing in the spirit, he could see the spirit of fear five miles away.

Here's another story. This one is about overcoming fear. A minister friend of our family, Judson Cornwall, told this story in one of his sermons. He had been dealing with some type of spiritual "captivity." The Lord had shown him he was in a jail cell (not in reality). Every time he tried to leave the cell, he would hear the roar of a lion and shrink back into the cell. The Lord told Judson on this occasion that He was opening the door for the last time. If Judson did not leave the cell, the door was going to permanently close. Of course, he did not want to stay locked in there, but then he heard the roar of the lion. He could not go back, so he had to press forward. He knew the lion was between him and total freedom. He moved forward until he got to the door and heard the roar on the other side. He knew he had to face it. He opened the door and there on the floor was a tape recorder with the sound of the roar of a lion. All this time, he had cowered in fear to a sound, not an actual lion. This makes sense because the devil is an "as a." He goes about AS A roaring lion—he's not really one. There's only one roaring lion and it's the Lion of the Tribe of Judah—Jesus Christ.

God wants us to be free—naturally and spiritually.

How do we deal with these spirits? Let's see how God empowers us.

LOOSE HIM AND LET HIM GO

We are spirit, have a soul and live in a body. Our spirit has been made alive unto God. It is the spirit man that we want directing our lives.

> *"...Walk in the Spirit, and you shall not fulfill the lust of the flesh"* (Galatians 5:16).

As we feed our spirits, the flesh takes less and less prominence.

Our spirits are saved and made alive unto God, not our flesh. We are transformed because our minds are renewed, not because we control our sin. Satan has no entrance to our spirits because we are washed and protected by the powerful, strong, holding blood of the Lord Jesus Christ, the only perfect Lamb of God. His plan is to affect our flesh and soul (mind, will and emotions). Unfortunately, our flesh wars against our spirit. The trauma he wants to wreak can be lifelong and generational, BUT we have the power of the Holy Spirit, the Kingdom of God, the weapons of our warfare, and armor of God to work in us and on our behalf.

Jesus has:

1) Destroyed the works of the enemy
2) Made us a new creation
3) Accepted us
4) Seated us in heavenly places
5) Given us all things that pertain to life and godliness
6) Given us weapons of warfare
7) Imparted the power of the Holy Spirit
8) Given us the armor of God

That's great, but if we don't use them, it is like sitting in our house with a tank in our front yard. We go out and polish the tank making a grand show of it to the neighbors. It keeps those punk thieves away because they are just looking for opportunity. The petty thieves are not coming—it's too risky. But the sophisticated, prideful thief will want to know what must be in our house that is so great we have to keep a tank in the front yard. The tank only acts as an invitation. The weapons are to be used.

Read what Jesus says in Matthew (twice):

> *"And I will give you the keys of the kingdom of heaven, and whatever you bind on earth will be bound in heaven, and*

> *whatever you loose on earth will be loosed in heaven"*
> (Matthew 16:19).

> *"Assuredly, I say to you, whatever you bind on earth will be bound in heaven, and whatever you loose on earth will be loosed in heaven"* (Matthew 18:18).

Look what David said God does:

> *"...He brings out those who are bound into prosperity;..."*
> (Psalm 68:6).

God wants us free. Let's do what Jesus said—bind and loose on earth, then the heavens will be bound and loosed. We believe Jesus so it leads us to obedience. Let's do it!

Prayer:

> In the name of Jesus, we cancel every demonic assignment against us and our family. We condemn the words of the accuser of the brethren. We loose everything You have for us. We live under an open heaven and upon an open earth. Our prayers are heard and our harvests are plentiful. As we are freed, we become freedom fighters to set the captives free! Thank You, Lord, for Your love for us! Amen.

Chapter Eleven

Setting People Free

We must be open to God giving us revelation. Sometimes, the things or way He wants us to do things are not the conventional or religious way to which we are accustomed. Jesus told the disciples He had more things to say, but they weren't ready yet. He was going to send the Holy Spirit who would be their teacher. We can always learn from our circumstances, but our teacher is the Holy Spirit who leads us into all truth. Jesus was adamant that He had to leave so the Holy Spirit could come.

Remember the story of Peter praying on the rooftop? Three times, God let down a sheet with unclean animals saying, "Eat." This was against everything Peter had been taught. These dietary laws had been observed since Moses, but God was preparing Peter to go to the Gentiles where they could eat everything, except that which they knew had been offered to idols. Didn't that challenge Peter? Yes!

Jesus came so we could be free. As He frees us, we then, in turn, free others!

POUR IN THE OIL AND WINE

These truths can be used for ourselves and for others.

We pour in the oil and wine of the Holy Ghost. This is in the story of the good Samaritan:

> *"He stooped down and gave him first aid, pouring olive oil on his wounds, disinfecting them with wine, and bandaging them to stop the bleeding..."* (Luke 10:34 TPT).

We pour in the oil for cleansing and wine for disinfecting. We bind up any wounds left by the enemy with the oil and wine of the Holy Ghost to bring wholeness to our lives.

> *"He heals the brokenhearted And binds up their wounds"* (Psalm 147:3).

> *"And you shall know the truth, and the truth shall make you free"* (John 8:32).

The truth liberates us!

WHAT DO WE BIND?

1) **We bind ourselves to the love of God.** It is the perfect love of God which casts out all fear.

    > *"...perfect love casts out fear, because fear involves torment. But he who fears has not been made perfect in love. We love Him because He first loved us"* (I John 4:18-19).

    This scripture is not about our perfect love toward God because we don't have perfect love. He has perfect love toward us. Can we love the Lord our God with all our heart, all our soul and all our strength? No, but Jesus did!

2) **We bind ourselves to the Kingdom of God**, which is righteousness, peace and joy.

> *"for the kingdom of God is not eating and drinking, but righteousness and peace and joy in the Holy Spirit"* (Romans 14:17).

He gives us peace that passes all understanding.

> *"and the peace of God, which surpasses all understanding, will guard your hearts and minds through Christ Jesus"* (Philippians 4:7).

The joy of the Lord is our strength.

> *"...for the joy of the LORD is your strength"* (Nehemiah 8:10).

We have His gift of righteousness, His peace that passes all understanding and strength because we have His joy.

SHALOM

"Shalom" is a Jewish greeting. Brian Simmons, who was involved in bringing about The Passion Translation of the Bible, describes the word "shalom" this way:

> SHALOM means much more than peace. It is wholeness, wellness, and well-being. It is safe, happy and friendly. It is favor and completeness. It means to make peace (a peace offering), to secure, to prosper, to be victorious and to be content. It is tranquil, quiet and restful...
> The pictographic symbols for the word "shalom" (shin, lamed, vav, mem) read: "Destroy the authority that binds to chaos." The noun "shalom" is derived from the verbal root "shalam," which means "to restore" (in the sense of replacing or providing what is

needed in order to make someone or something whole and complete).

In the Old Testament, when God said an eye for an eye and a tooth for a tooth, these were not revenge laws. These were shalom scriptures—nothing missing, nothing broken. He wanted people whole. The intent was this: if someone caused us to be broken in any way or missing anything, then that person needed to replace it to keep us whole. God does the same for us now. He wants nothing missing or broken in us. He wants us whole.

3) **We bind ourselves to the callings and destinies of God.** We will fulfill that which God has called us to and for which He has purposed us.

> *"For I know the thoughts that I think toward you, says the LORD, thoughts of peace and not of evil, to give you a future and a hope"* (Jeremiah 29:11).

> *"We have become his poetry, a re-created people that will fulfill the destiny he has given each of us, for we are joined to Jesus, the Anointed One. Even before we were born, God planned in advance our destiny and the good works we would do to fulfill it!"*
> (Ephesians 2:10 TPT).

We have built our house on the Rock, so no matter what shaking goes on, we are securely and firmly in Him.

We do all the binding toward God and His Kingdom, cleansing and disinfecting wounds for healing so Satan has nothing to hang on to (trauma, wounds) when we loose him. We don't want him finding a clean house to keep residence (Luke 11:26).

LOOSING

We loose ourselves from any way the enemy has put his claws in our lives, whether they are embedded now or have left festering woundedness. Woundedness is not just remembering an event; woundedness is still feeling like it happened yesterday. It's still raw. Or maybe the trauma caused us to set up fences and roadblocks by which we have been incarcerated ever since. Instead of imprisoning ourselves, why don't we tell the enemy to go to hell?

We resist every attempt for the enemy to work in our lives. We renounce any way that we have agreed with Satan, whether known or unknown. We take away any permission given, whether purposefully or inadvertently.

James 4:7 says:

"...submit to God. Resist the devil and he will flee from you."

We have submitted to God because we are doing what Jesus said—to bind and loose. The devil has to flee!!

BE SET FREE!

Let's summarize this:

1) Take away the stone – we don't have to be in trauma anymore. Those things that have rotted and are stinking can be let go.
2) Pour in the oil and wine – cleaning and disinfecting.
3) Bind oneself to the love of God.
4) Bind oneself to the Kingdom of God.
5) Bind oneself to the purposes of God.
6) Loose any way the enemy has claws in us, whether current or festering wounds.

Holy Spirit, we thank You that You have liberated us from our captivity and are healing us so we may be whole. Thank You that our spiritual senses are activated. Keep a watch over us. Alert us to trauma the enemy wants to bring or utilize to get a foot in the door of our hearts. Refresh us with Your truth. Reveal any secret accords that have been made. We thank You for loving us and calling us forth. We are loosed and we go free. Amen!

Listen to the Holy Spirit. He may lead us to do this for several days and/or weeks. He may bring us back to it again as the enemy has launched fresh assaults against us. I have experienced real healing through this.

The Holy Spirit may also bring other things to our attention. For example, since I've done this binding and loosing, He has had me release any guardians that are not of God. The enemy wants to deceive us. We release them from "protecting" us from hearing and perceiving truth.

THE TRAUMA OF JESUS

Lest we think the enemy only comes after us, he used the same tactics against Jesus. When the enemy wants to bring trauma, it may be through emotional ways or even physical ways. It's his way to pry open the door for anger, bitterness, fear, wrath, etc. Look what the enemy did to Jesus in physical ways to bring trauma:

- Jesus was wounded and beaten, but it brought forth the forgiveness of our transgressions.
- Jesus was bruised, which is blood beneath the skin, but it brought forth healing for our emotional wounds (can't be seen).
- Jesus was chastised, but it made Him our peace.

- Jesus was striped with whips, but it brought forth healing for us.
- Jesus had a crown of thorns pushed into his scalp, but it purchased the healing for our minds.
- Jesus was nailed to a cross, but He became a curse so curses would not hold against us.
- The hands of Jesus were nailed to the cross so now His blood covers the work of our hands.
- The feet of Jesus were nailed to the cross so now His blood covers wherever we go.
- Jesus was forsaken. He cried out asking God why He had been forsaken. He was forsaken so we could be accepted.
- Jesus was murdered because He was innocent of everything, but He paid the price for us. Instead of hatred, forgiveness flowed.

"…Father, forgive them, for they do not know what they do" (Luke 23:34).

- Jesus died at 33. He lived a short life so we could have a long life.

Instead of Satan bringing trauma by breaking open the body of Jesus, Jesus poured out redemption.

Just like Lazarus, the stone was put over the tomb of Jesus. Just like Lazarus, the stone was rolled away. Just like Lazarus, God called Jesus forth. Just like Lazarus, He was loosed and let go. (Through the raising of Lazarus, was God letting Jesus foresee how He was going to come forth out of the tomb?)

COMMUNION

> *"For as often as you eat this bread and drink this cup, you proclaim the Lord's death till He comes."*
> (I Corinthians 11:26).

In olden times, warriors would sit around regaling stories of the brave and heroic who may or may not have survived battles. It was a way to remind them of victory, but also the cost of that victory.

Communion is the way we remember and proclaim the victory of our Lord Jesus Christ over death, hell and the grave. The crucifixion gave Him victory over death and hell, but His resurrection gave Him victory over the grave, as well. This victory proves He was the Lamb of God and that His precious, perfect blood was accepted by God in Heaven.

> *"And if Christ is not risen, your faith is futile; you are still in your sins!"* (I Corinthians 15:17).

Jesus even warned them:

> *"...for if you do not believe that I am He, you will die in your sins"* (John 8:24).

If we don't believe His blood was accepted by the Father, there is no more blood being offered.

> *"...and without shedding of blood there is no remission"* (Hebrews 9:22).

HOW OFTEN SHOULD WE TAKE COMMUNION?

How often do we want to remember the victory of Jesus on the cross? How often do we want to proclaim His death—

winning victory over death, hell and the grave? We can take it as often as we would like.

Whenever we take it, remember His body was broken for us—for salvation, healing and redemption.

> *"...Take, eat; this is My body which is broken for you; do this in remembrance of Me"* (I Corinthians 11:24).

Take the cup of the New Covenant. His blood was shed for us, washing away (not covering) our sin.

> *"...This cup is the new covenant in My blood. This do, as often as you drink it, in remembrance of Me. For as often as you eat this bread and drink this cup, you proclaim the Lord's death till He comes"* (I Corinthians 11:25-26).

Paul does not tell us we have to take communion in church only. We can partake at home by ourselves or with our family or with friends.

Liberators – We have been liberated to set others free! Here are more liberation scriptures:

- ➢ Liberation from the world's way of thinking and doing—bondage.

  > *"And do not be conformed to this world, but be transformed by the renewing of your mind, that you may prove what is that good and acceptable and perfect will of God"* (Romans 12:2).

- ➢ Liberation from strongholds, arguments and every high thing that exalts itself.

  > *"For the weapons of our warfare are not carnal but mighty in God for pulling down strongholds, casting down arguments and every high thing that exalts itself*

against the knowledge of God, bringing every thought into captivity to the obedience of Christ,"
(II Corinthians 10:4-5).

➢ Liberation from our thoughts and feelings controlling us.

"For the word of God is…piercing even to the division of soul and spirit, and of joints and marrow, and is a discerner of the thoughts and intents of the heart"
(Hebrews 4:12).

➢ Liberation from darkness and sin.

"He has delivered us from the power of darkness and conveyed us into the kingdom of the Son of His love, in whom we have redemption through His blood, the forgiveness of sins" (Colossians 1:13-14).

➢ Liberation from grief and destruction.

"To console those who mourn…To give them beauty for ashes, The oil of joy for mourning, The garment of praise for the spirit of heaviness…" (Isaiah 61:3).

Section V

Manifesting Christians

Chapter Twelve

From Old to New

Imagine a scene. It was crazy by many standards, but this was excitement. Not excitement that leads to mobs of crime and violence, but hordes of people excited about good things that are happening. They've heard about this, but now they are actually in the midst of it. One man was in the forefront—Jesus!

> *"Then great multitudes came to Him, having with them the lame, blind, mute, maimed, and many others; and they laid them down at Jesus' feet, and He healed them"* (Matthew 15:30).

This was not an isolated happening:

> *"But when Jesus knew it, He withdrew from there. And great multitudes followed Him, and He healed them ALL."* (Matthew 12:15) (emphasis mine).

> *"And great multitudes followed Him, and He healed them there"* (Matthew 19:2).

> *"Then the blind and the lame came to Him in the temple, and He healed them"* (Matthew 21:14).

> *"And the WHOLE multitude sought to touch Him, for power went out from Him and healed them ALL"* (Luke 6:19) (emphasis mine).

> *"Then His fame went throughout all Syria; and they brought to Him ALL sick people who were afflicted with various diseases and torments, and those who were demon-possessed, epileptics, and paralytics; and He healed them"*
> (Matthew 4:24) (emphasis mine).

Let's continue with this crazy scene. People who had been lame walked and jumped and were yelling to their loved ones and friends, "LOOK, I'M WALKING. NOW, I CAN RUN!" Mothers wept and exclaimed, "MY BABY CAN SEE!" Deaf people yelled asking people to "SAY SOMETHING, ANYTHING..." The maimed grabbed their friends saying, "LOOK AT MY ARM! IT GREW BACK. I CAN WORK. I CAN PROVIDE FOR MY FAMILY!" The mute excitedly talked plainly and OUT LOUD, without the pitiful stares from onlookers, trying not to gesture with their hands because now they had audible words.

How wonderful that must have been! What joy that must have brought Jesus to see people made whole! Remember, His desire is that we have nothing missing, nothing broken!

THE PURPOSE OF JESUS – FULFILLED

The Bible tells us why Jesus came:

> *"...For this purpose the Son of God was manifested, that He might destroy the works of the devil"* (I John 3:8).

> *"...But now he has appeared at the fulfillment of the age to abolish sin once and for all by the sacrifice of himself!"*
> (Hebrews 9:26 TPT).

Mission accomplished. Sin dealt with.

> *"And you, being dead in your trespasses and the uncircumcision of your flesh, HE HAS MADE alive together with Him, <u>having forgiven you ALL trespasses</u>, having wiped out the handwriting of requirements that was against us...And He has taken it out of the way, having nailed it to the cross. Having disarmed principalities and power, He made a public spectacle of them, triumphing over them in it"* (Colossians 2:13-15) (emphasis mine).

If we have received Christ, we have been forgiven. We no longer take out the microscope and look for sin. The Holy Spirit convicts us of our righteousness. If we've missed the mark, He will lead us to repent, and we turn. Trust the Holy Spirit. The Bible tells us to "look up" for our redemption. The devil wants us to continually gaze at our navel—looking at our faults and weaknesses. When we do that, we never see anything good. The devil wants us looking at what he's done, not what Christ has done!

THE END OF ONE AND BEGINNING OF ANOTHER

Jesus was not a replacement for the law. Jesus fulfilled the law and finalized the Old Covenant, ushering in the New Covenant with His crucifixion, death and resurrection.

> *"But now He has obtained a more excellent ministry, inasmuch as He is also Mediator of a better covenant, which was established on better promises"* (Hebrews 8:6).

> *"This proves that by establishing this new covenant the first is now obsolete, ready to expire, and about to disappear"* (Hebrews 8:13 TPT).

The dividing of the Bible into the Old Testament and New Testament is not the division of the two covenants. Jesus lived and worked under the Old Covenant. It wasn't until His blood was received by the Father, proven by His resurrection from the dead and His ascension, that the New Covenant came into play. So, the New Covenant is shown coming forth with the Book of Acts.

Chapter Thirteen

Holy Spirit

IT'S ADVANTAGEOUS

Now that Jesus has shown us what a human can be like working under the anointing of the Holy Spirit, He made a way for this same Spirit to dwell in us. In the Old Testament, the Holy Spirit would come upon someone, but didn't dwell in them. Because of the death and resurrection of Jesus, and us becoming new creations, the Holy Spirit can now come and abide in us.

The Holy Spirit must be important as Jesus told the disciples that it was to their advantage that He was leaving so the Holy Spirit could come.

> *"Nevertheless I tell you the truth. It is to your advantage that I go away; for if I do not go away, the Helper will not come to you; but if I depart, I will send Him to you...I still have many things to say to you, but you cannot bear them now. However, when He, the Spirit of truth, has come, He will guide you into all truth; for He will not speak on His own authority, but whatever He hears He will speak; and He will tell you things to come"* (John 16:7,12-13).

If the reason Jesus was able to perform the works that He did was because He was the Son of God, why did He have to be anointed?

> *"how God anointed Jesus of Nazareth with the Holy Spirit and with power, who went about doing good and healing ALL who were oppressed by the devil, for God was with Him"* (Acts 10:38) (emphasis mine).

He became poor (human) so that we could be rich—spirit, soul and body. Jesus manifested the Spirit and we have the same Spirit dwelling in and quickening our mortal bodies.

> *"But if the Spirit of Him who raised Jesus from the dead dwells in you, He who raised Christ from the dead will also give life to your mortal bodies through His Spirit who dwells in you"* (Romans 8:11).

This wasn't just a funky, next-spiritual-fad kind of thing. This was the power of the Kingdom. This was Who was going to lead us into being like Jesus all over the world. This was Who was going to guide us into all truth and tell us of things to come.

After His resurrection, Jesus instructed those watching His ascension:

> *"Behold, I send the Promise of My Father upon you; but tarry in the city of Jerusalem until you are endued with power from on high"* (Luke 24:49).

It belittles the Holy Spirit to refer to Him as our "prayer language." Jesus did not instruct them to get a prayer language. He said the Promise of God was coming and they would be endued with POWER. He has come to endue us with POWER and to give us MANIFESTATIONS. The Holy Spirit is power—not like a birthday candle, but like an exploding piece of dynamite!

SUPERNATURAL MANIFESTATIONS

When we are a Christian, it's natural to be supernatural and it is not natural if we aren't. Sounds crazy, doesn't it? Yet, it bears witness. Look what happened in Acts chapter 2 when the Holy Spirit came:

> *"And suddenly there came a sound from heaven, as of a rushing mighty wind, and it filled the whole house where they were sitting. Then there appeared to them divided tongues, as of fire, and one sat upon each of them. And they were all filled with the Holy Spirit and began to speak with other tongues, as the Spirit gave then utterance…And when this sound occurred, the multitude came together, and were confused, because everyone heard them speak in his own language. Then they were all amazed and marveled, saying to one another, 'Look, are not all these who speak Galileans? And how is it that we hear, each in our own language in which were born? Parthians and Medes and Elamites, those dwelling in Mesopotamia, Judea and Cappadocia, Pontus and Asia, Phrygia and Pamphylia, Egypt and the parts of Libya adjoining Cyrene, visitors from Rome, both Jews and proselytes, Cretans and Arabs—we hear them speaking in our own tongues the wonderful works of God'"* (Acts 2:2-11).

We think far below our Kingdom citizenship if we think Jesus and the Holy Spirit came for us to live and worship God like mere men! The Kingdom is about power. Paul said:

> *"For our gospel did not come to you in word only, but also in power, and in the Holy Spirit and in much assurance…"*
> (I Thessalonians 1:5).

> *"For the kingdom of God is not in word but in power"*
> (I Corinthians 4:20).

God did not send His only begotten Son to destroy the works of the devil only for us to be good humans.

> *"...For this purpose the Son of God was manifested, that He might destroy the works of the devil"* (I John 3:8).

God did not send His Holy Spirit to dwell in us—the same Spirit that raised Christ from the dead only for us to be good humans.

> *"But if the Spirit of Him who raised Jesus from the dead dwells in you, He who raised Christ from the dead will also give life to your mortal bodies through His Spirit who dwells in you"* (Romans 8:11).

God did not send His Spirit that endues us with power only for us to be good humans.

> *"Behold, I send the Promise of My Father upon you; but tarry in the city of Jerusalem until you are endued with power from on high"* (Luke 24:49).

God did not send this power that demonstrates the Kingdom of God only for us to be good humans.

> *"For the kingdom of God is not in word but in power"* (I Corinthians 4:20).

Let me repeat that: God did not send His only begotten Son to destroy the works of the devil only for us to be good humans. God did not send His Holy Spirit to dwell in us—the same Spirit that raised Christ from the dead—only for us to be good humans. God did not send His Spirit that endues us with power only for us to be good humans. God did not send this power that demonstrates the Kingdom of God only for us to be good humans.

If our Christian walk is one we can do because we have a little fortitude, a good attitude and a sunny disposition, then we are walking in the flesh. People without God can do that.

> *"O foolish Galatians! Who has bewitched you…Are you so foolish? Having begun in the Spirit, are you now being made perfect by the flesh?"* (Galatians 3:1,3).

RELIGIOUS SPIRIT

A religious spirit is like Jabba the Hutt in "Return of the Jedi," one of the Star Wars movies. Jabba was a big, fat, slimy warlord. This religious spirit wants to sit on us, pulling a dimness over our eyes. Any time we have a revelation or see something of God that causes faith to arise for deliverance or miraculous change in our situation, his sickeningly smooth, silky voice says, "Now, now. Settle down. No reason to get so excited. Into every life a little rain must fall! When life hands you lemons, make lemonade!" One of the manifestations of the Holy Spirit is discerning of spirits. In the power and name of Jesus, our Lord and Savior, we overthrow that spirit and give it no place and no attention.

VEIL OVER OUR EYES?

The Word says that when the law of Moses is read, there is a veil over our eyes, but the veil is removed for us when we are saved. BUT if we go back to living by the law, are we not giving permission for the veil to be put back over our eyes?

> *"Therefore, since we have such hope, we use great boldness of speech—unlike Moses, who put a veil over his face so that the children of Israel could not look steadily at the end of what was passing away. But their minds were blinded. For until this day the same veil remains unlifted in the reading of the Old*

Testament, because the veil is taken away in Christ. But even to this day, when Moses is read, a veil lies on their heart. Nevertheless when one turns to the Lord, the veil is taken away" (II Corinthians 3:12-16).

WHAT IS JESUS LIKE?

We spend time with Him because we get to know Him. What does He smell like? Jesus was called the Rose of Sharon. What does He sound like?

"My sheep hear My voice, and I know them, and they follow Me" (John 10:27).

"…His voice as the sound of many waters;" (Revelation 1:15).

God is real.

GOD IS NOT AN IDOL

One time, God said to me, "Do not make Me an idol!" What? I thought an idol was a graven image, something we make with our hands.

Let's see what Psalm 135 defines as an idol:

"…They have mouths, but they do not speak; Eyes they have, but they do not see; They have ears, but they do not hear; Nor is there any breath in their mouths. Those who make them are like them; So is everyone who trusts in them" (Psalm 135:15-18).

Does God speak to us? Do we expect Him to? Does God tell us what He sees? Does He show us? Do we believe God hears our prayers? Do we hear Him? Are we okay to pray forever with no answer?

Praying just to "pray" or check off a religious box is futile. This leads us to believe God heard us, but then because we are just going through the motions and no answer comes, we flip and believe God did not hear us. Then, our prayers become religious duty. Next, we might develop a victim mentality with the belief, "look how I'm suffering for Christ." Then, we believe no answer is okay. See the downward progression? The next logical conclusion is to ask, "Is God even alive?" See where the "world" lives?

If we answer "no" to any of those questions, we better check our god—little "g." We might have just turned Him into an idol, not believing He hears, speaks or sees!

While we may believe it's okay to have no answers to prayer and no live interaction with God, what makes anyone else want to come to that god? People without God live without their situations changing. They don't need a god idol for the same hopelessness as people who don't have the one true God.

SEEKING MANIFESTATIONS

We do not seek manifestations to make us believe, but because we believe and are filled with the Spirit, we look for the manifestations. We don't look for signs and wonders. They are supposed to follow us, but if they're not following us, let's ask, "Why, Lord?"

Is it wrong to question God? This is not questioning God in unbelief. This shows Him we believe His Word. If we went to the grocery store and the butcher told us he was selling the best, most tender cut of beef and then we went home and it was tough and full of fat, wouldn't we go back and ask the butcher about it? Because we believed the butcher, we would ask why it wasn't as he said.

If we go to the doctor and he prescribes medicine, but it doesn't work, don't we go back to the doctor to ask for a different medicine because the prescription isn't working? Do we believe the butcher and doctor more than we believe God? Do we expect answers to our prayers? Don't we expect our prayers to work?

When the enemy comes and whispers in our ear and tells us that "no one has seen what you are asking for," "that's impossible," "it's never been done," "it will never happen," our response is "LIAR!!" I'M PRAYING TO GOD! He's not "A" good god, as one of many. He is "THE" one and only God and He's "THE" good, loving, merciful, forgiving, supplying, healing, prayer-answering God!!! He's our perfect, heavenly Father and He is not like anyone we've ever met and certainly not like any human, that He should lie!!!

DO WE TRUST GOD?

A few years ago, God asked me, "Do you trust Me?" I pondered this question and how to answer it. I knew the "correct" answer was, "Yes, of course, God," but in reality, I had to say, "No, I don't." Gasp! Yet, it was like God said, "Honesty! I can work with that."

After some time, I realized I really trusted God. It wasn't like something had drastically changed in my life or some long-awaited answer to prayer had arrived. God had just worked in me and I knew I trusted Him. So, happily, as I was riding along in my car one day, I will never forget it, I informed God that I now trusted Him. (Wasn't that magnanimous of me?) God's answer? "It's not that you trust Me. It's that I AM trustworthy!"

If He is trustworthy, then we can ask why His Word isn't working as He said. Have we missed it? Is there demonic activity and delay at work in the situation? After all, we don't want to be "waiting" when we're supposed to use our authority in some capacity, but we do want to wait when we're tempted to run ahead of Him. Don't you love how God can correct us without condemning us?

After the day of Pentecost when the Holy Spirit fell, we see where Peter's shadow would fall upon the sick and they would be healed. They prayed over cloths and took them and laid them on sick and demonized people and they were healed and delivered. They cast out demons. It was so demonstrative that Simon the sorcerer wanted to pay to have their power. This is the same Holy Spirit we have.

FROM GLORY TO GLORY

We are already acquainted with the power of God. When we got saved, it was not just an arbitrary decision, but a bold act of faith to believe that we could be released from the power of the kingdom of darkness and brought into the kingdom of His beautiful Son!! Two powers at work, sin and death or everlasting life, but the power of our God is much greater and is no comparison to the other power.

> *"For I am not ashamed of the gospel of Christ, for it is the power of God to salvation for everyone who believes..."*
> (Romans 1:16) (emphasis mine).

> *"He has delivered us from the power of darkness and conveyed us into the kingdom of the Son of His love, in whom we have redemption through His blood, the forgiveness of sins"*
> (Colossians 1:13-14).

Once we are saved, then we grow and move in the Kingdom of God. Jesus told the disciples He had more to tell them but needed to tell them through the Holy Spirit. If true for the disciples, isn't it true for us, as well? We may not be one of the original 12, but we are disciples of Christ, aren't we? If we buy into the deception that only Jesus, because He was the begotten Son of God, or the original 12 disciples could move in the kind of power we read about in Acts, then we have bought into a non-mountain-moving, non-life-changing, non-earth-shaking, non-kingdom-of-darkness-challenging religion that believes we can just smile at people and that will bless their lives. Where did we ever have that example?

Chapter Fourteen

Manifestation

Why should the demonic have the privilege of manifesting in the earth? We read in one of the earlier chapters that God gave the earth to the children of men. The earth is for us, not the demons. Jesus constantly told the demons to be quiet. Notice, He didn't have to call out to the demons—they called out to Him.

Let us, as Holy Spirit filled children of the Most High God, manifest His wonderful power in the earth. This is not only for us, but to give hope to those without hope, for us to be the liberators discussed in the last section.

Romans 8:26 says:

> *"Likewise the Spirit also helps in our weaknesses. For we do not know what we should pray for as we ought, but the Spirit Himself makes intercession for us with groanings which cannot be uttered."*

According to this, aside from the Holy Spirit, we don't even know how to pray!

How does the Spirit manifest? What Paul says in I Corinthians 12 is in no way a comprehensive list. Just as God never led the children of Israel in the same way (only one Red Sea parting, only one Jericho, only one time the wind blew in the mulberry trees, only one Gideon, only one time they dug ditches, etc.), the Spirit moves in many ways. It is our privilege to know Him and His ways to move in whatever situation we are in, in whatever way He says. This was what God admired in David when the Scriptures said he had a heart after God.

Look at the story of David at Ziklag in I Samuel 30. After David and his army return from an arduous battle, they find that the town of Ziklag where they lived had been plundered and all their families and possessions were gone. David didn't assume he would get it all back. He sought the Lord and God told him to pursue and recover all. We don't always operate in the same repetitive way, but in whatever way or however the Spirit wants to lead.

> *"But the MANIFESTATION of the Spirit is given to each one for the profit of all: for to one is given the word of wisdom through the Spirit, to another the word of knowledge through the same Spirit, to another faith by the same Spirit, to another gifts of healings by the same Spirit, to another the working of miracles, to another prophecy, to another discerning of spirits, to another different kinds of tongues, to another the interpretation of tongues"*
> (I Corinthians 12:7-10) (emphasis mine).

These can be broken down into three different kinds of gifts:

Revelatory
- Word of wisdom
- Word of knowledge
- Discerning of spirits

Utterance
- Tongues
- Interpretation of tongues
- Prophecy

Power
- Faith
- Gifts of healings
- Working of miracles

Jesus walked in the manifestation of the Spirit. Remember, He became poor—being fully God, but choosing to live as a human—to be like us. He showed us how we, as humans, could walk in the anointing of the Spirit. How did the Holy Spirit work through Jesus? The same Holy Spirit that anointed Jesus anoints us (this is not an exhaustive study):

1) <u>Words of Wisdom</u> – the parables; the woman caught in adultery.
2) <u>Words of Knowledge</u> – the woman at the well; money in the mouth of the fish; telling Peter to cast the net on the other side of the boat for a boatload of fish; sending the disciples to prepare for the last supper and telling them they would find a donkey.
3) <u>Discerning of Spirits</u> – Peter said Jesus was the Christ, the Son of the living God and Jesus said that revelation didn't come from flesh and blood, but from the Father. Later, when Peter chided Jesus over talking about His death, Jesus said, "Get behind Me, Satan!" Jesus was discerning spirits by the manifestation of the Holy Spirit in Him! In Mark 5, Jesus meets the man of Gadera with a legion of demons (demons never come alone). It would seem discerning of spirits is unnecessary when the demons are screeching, but some would have just thought he was crazy. The supernatural works so "naturally" at times, it is not discerned—whether it is God working or the demonic is manifesting.

Jesus was not omniscient (all knowing) while He was on the earth. He only knew what God told Him. This was part of His "becoming poor that we might be rich." Everything He did was through the power of the Holy Ghost, which is how the Kingdom works through us!

Jesus marveled at people's faith. If He would have "known" they were going to show that faith, He wouldn't have marveled at it. If He knew it already and the Scripture says He marveled when He was only pretending, then the Scripture is being manipulative and we know the Scripture is not manipulative! Manipulation is a 'soft' form of witchcraft.

Also, omniscience is an attribute of God. Omnipresence is also an attribute of God. Jesus was not omnipresent (in all places at one time) as people had to go where He was. Therefore, Jesus was not omniscient on earth.

4) <u>Prophecy</u> – Peter, upon this rock I will build my church (Matthew 16); destruction of the temple, the signs of the end of the age, the Tribulation, and His second coming (Matthew 24).

5) <u>Faith</u> – *"without faith it is impossible to please Him"* (Hebrews 11:6). God would not have said to Jesus at His baptism He was pleased if Jesus didn't walk by faith. *"This is My beloved Son, in whom I am well pleased"* (Matthews 3:17). All He did—miracles, healing, delivering, prophesying, and teaching—was through faith.

6) <u>Gifts of Healing</u> – the blind, the lame, lepers, woman with the issue of blood, epileptics, paralytics, the mute, the maimed…

7) <u>Working of Miracles</u> – multiplying the bread and fish and feeding the 5,000, turning water into wine, calming the storm, walking through crowds that

wanted to stone him and throw Him over a cliff, raising the dead, walking on water…

The same Holy Spirit that anointed Jesus anoints us! This is what Jesus did that we can't:

1) Die for the sins of the world.
2) Present our blood to the Father to wash sin away, not cover it like the blood of bulls and goats.
3) Be resurrected so that all men and women, who accept what He has done, can walk in that resurrection.

We cannot do these things for ourselves, much less for all of mankind. The interesting thing is we try to do what only He can do (pay for our sin), but we don't think we are worthy to walk in the gifts of the Spirit that He not only told us to, but which the Father sent as a gift to us. Remember Hebrews 3:12? Unbelief makes us unresponsive to the voice of the living God.

The era we are moving into is one that is going to require manifestations of the Spirit in and through us. We cannot afford to act like the Kingdom is just a cafeteria line and we pick and choose what we want and don't want. "I'll have salvation, but that's all I want." No, let's be hungry and take all of it. The Spirit can then dish out what He wants us to have when He wants us to have it. He wants us walking in the fullness of the Spirit.

The Word tells us that "all of creation" groans for the manifestation of the sons of God (Romans 8:19). We need to get past an "only human" paradigm. The Word says the trees clap their hands, the rocks cry out, the manifestation of calming the winds and seas ministers to the fish and birds as much as the humans. What about stopping fires or earthquakes and volcanoes? Genesis 9:15 tells us the covenant of never flooding the earth again was between God, man and every living creature. God gave man dominion over all creation.

Chapter Fifteen

Spiritual Hunger

Spiritual hunger is one of the greatest things God can bless us with. Going to church every time the doors are open is good, but if it's just a meeting where the saints get together, it's not good enough! What about reading the Word? Pull that one verse from the little bread box—better than nothing, but not enough! It's not how much we read the Bible, but what did He say? Praying is good, but prayer time is not enough if God isn't speaking. We want Him.

Hunger drives us to go after Him. The Word says He will draw near to us if we draw near to Him! His Word says He will do many things with us and for us. If He didn't mean it, He should not have said it because we take Him at His Word.

METHOD OF PRAYER CHANGED

Hunger has changed the way I pray. I used to pray about people to God. Now, I pray to God about people. A play on words? No. For example, my old prayer may have gone something like this: "God, I pray for Joe. Lord, He needs to make the right decisions. Help him make the right decisions and guide his path."

Now, I pray, "God, You created Joe. You know the giftings and callings You have placed in him. You know the plans You have for him. You are God. Encounter Joe!!! You know the things that will get his attention. You know what speaks to him. Be God in his life!!!!"

Can we see the difference? Instead of expecting Joe to do right and make right decisions, we ask God to encounter and manifest in Joe's life. One puts all the power in the person's hand. The other recognizes that God is all powerful. If He encountered the legalistic, murdering Saul and turned him into a powerhouse for God, He can still do the same today.

God made a donkey talk. The wind and waves obeyed Moses. Birds fed prophets. Birds told battle plans to prophets. Seas backed up. Walls fell down. A hand wrote on the wall. An iron axe head floated. A 1,000,000-man army coming against Israel turned and went back home. An angel slew 185,000 men. Commandments were written on stone tablets. Joseph was lifted out of prison to be second in the land. Esther and the Jews were saved from destruction. Protection in the form of a pillar of fire by night and a pillar of cloud by day kept the children of Israel through the wilderness. Manna dropped six mornings out of every week for 40 years and stopped the day they entered the promised land. A shepherd boy killed a giant. Childless couples received children. Indebted mothers received abundance to save their children. Four lepers saved a city. These are just a few of the miracles that happened under the Old Covenant before the Spirit was poured out. What could the New Covenant, which is a better covenant made on better promises, have in store for us?

THIS IS UNBELIEVABLE!!!

Rabbit Testimony

I heard a story about a man who got saved because his rabbit talked to him.

Fish Teach

A missionary told the story of how he was going to a village to preach the gospel. There was no way to get to the village except by boat so he went to a nearby village with boats. He asked if he could get to the village where he wanted to preach. They directed him to the fishermen down on the pier saying they could take him there because they were from that village. He went to the fishermen and told them he needed to go to their village. They asked him why? He said he wanted to come and tell them about Jesus. Their response, "We already know Jesus!" Shocked, the missionary asked, "How do you know? No one has been to your village." They responded, "When we fish at night, the fish jump out of the sea and tell us about Jesus."

"But now ask the beasts, and they will teach you; And the birds of the air, and they will tell you; Or speak to the earth, and it will teach you; And the fish of the sea will explain to you" (Job 12:7-8).

Oil Platform to Jungle

A man was walking across an oil platform in the ocean and "stepped" into a jungle. He was shocked by his new surroundings and the sight of a young man. He preached the gospel to the young man, but then they heard shouts coming through the brush. The young man told him to "run" and as he ran back into the jungle, he ran "onto" the platform. The man studied soils as part of his profession, so he examined the soil on his shoes and was able to determine it was from somewhere in South America. Years later, he was at a church conference and a young man came up to him. He said, "You probably don't remember me, but you preached the gospel to me in the jungle years ago. Through that, I became a minister and now I preach the gospel." He asked, "By the way, where did you go that night?"

Going to a Foreign Nation

God told a man to go to a foreign country, but he had no money. God told him to go to the airport. He did. He checked at the counter, but there were no tickets in his name. No one approached him. He asked, "Okay God, what now?"

"Go in the restroom with your luggage."

He did. Once more, he asked, "Okay?"

"Go in the stall with your luggage."

Shocked but, in obedience, he went into the stall. "Okay, now what?"

"Open the door of the stall and walk out."

He did and he was in the foreign nation where God had told him to go.

Smith Wigglesworth

Smith Wigglesworth raised around 16 people from the dead. He would sometimes put their bodies against the wall and they would slide down. He would pick them up again and command them to live. They did!

John G. Lake

John G. Lake worked in Africa during a plague. They asked him why he was not getting sick. He took some of the froth off the mouth of someone who had just died and put it on his hand. He put it under a microscope and told them to look. They saw the germs of the plague die on his hands. While he ministered to the sick and raised them up, the plague died not affecting him.

St. Patrick

St. Patrick came against the Druids in Ireland. The Druids had influenced the king to shut down the fires lit on holy holidays/nights. St. Patrick defied that order and lit the fires. The Druids were out to kill St. Patrick and had the king send out soldiers looking for him. St. Patrick was traveling with five men and a young boy of about 12-years-old. As they were traveling the countryside, they saw the king's men go by, but the soldiers never stopped. When the soldiers got back to the king, they reported they had seen nothing on their journey except six deer and a fawn. God caused the soldiers to see St. Patrick and his companions as deer.

St. Patrick came to the village of Dublin where the king resided. Two of the king's children had just died. One from a sickness and the other had drowned. The king told St. Patrick if he could raise his children from the dead, he would serve his God. St. Patrick raised them both up. The king served St. Patrick's God delivering him out of the age of and from under the influence of the Druids.

Minister Protected

Friends of my grandparents were missionaries in the Dakotas—Paul and Margaret Walker. They were pioneers. A man's wife had been saved in one of Rev. Walker's meetings and the man wasn't happy about it. He came to church with a gun and pulled it out during a service pointing it at Rev. Walker. His wife, Margaret, under the power of the Holy Ghost, began to spin like a top. The man's arm froze. He was unable to pull the trigger. They took him home and he died several days later.

Holy Spirit Discernment

A minister was visiting a church and while on that platform, he heard a woman in the congregation speaking in tongues. He asked the pastor who she was. He said she was head of their intercessory prayer group. He told the pastor she was cursing the church. The pastor couldn't believe it. The visiting minister commanded the woman to speak in English what she had been "speaking in tongues." Indeed, she was speaking curses over that body of believers. Discernment needed!!

Face Restored

My great grandfather, who found his teeth on the bottom of the Chesapeake Bay, was dying. My great grandmother had cancer on her face. He told her he was about to die and to comfort her that he was with the Lord, there would be a sign: the cancer on her face was going to be gone. The next morning, the family went upstairs to tell her that granddad had died during the night. As she washed her face in the wash basin, the cancer fell off her face into her hand and fresh, baby-like skin was left where that cancer had been.

Doesn't this make us salivate? Don't we want to do and see these kinds of things too? These are not just things for "special people." These are things for all the people of God, but they are not in our own power.

If we can walk out our salvation in our own strength, we are missing what God has for us. He wants to work through us to do things we can never do as a mere human! I have been convicted of being in conventions and going to church all the time to learn "how" to be a Christian. It was all about me knowing how to do the "right thing" so my flesh can be right with God and I can "earn" His favor. This is religion pure and simple. People of God hear His voice and follow Him!

Religion does not walk by the Spirit and therefore cannot manifest the giftings of the Spirit! Religion makes us passive and powerless.

John 14:21 says:

> "...he who loves Me will be loved by My Father, and I will love him and manifest Myself to him."

Jesus said He would manifest Himself to us. Are we living in these privileges? Are we okay to walk only in what our flesh can do? I'm not. I'm hungry for Him!

For the fivefold ministry:

- Teachers: Don't just teach to teach but teach with authority and anointing that sees the Body of Christ established in truth!
- Pastors: Don't just be a good person leading a group but be an anointed pastor leading the sheep and nurturing them to lion-of-the-tribe-of-Judah likeness!
- Evangelists: Don't preach canned sermons on salvation but preach anointed sermons seeing the lost convicted by the Holy Ghost and getting saved and being powerfully set free from violence, drugs and any other addictions or agendas of the kingdom of darkness. Saul/Paul transformations.
- Prophets: Don't just give "bless me" prophecies like, "The Lord blesses you and loves you," but give words that lead and direct groups of people including confrontation of anti-God governmental authorities.
- Apostles: Don't just establish another "group" for a religious organization. Establish a Holy Ghost hub that sees regions changed for the Kingdom of God.

Chapter Sixteen

Take It

Several years ago, the Lord began to show me some things about myself. They were things "hidden" from my consciousness. He showed me I was waiting to be rewarded. Oh, I would never have said that out loud, but I was going about doing good and believing while waiting for the answers. I began to realize I was waiting to be rewarded. I wanted my faith to be rewarded. I wanted my waiting to be rewarded. I had unconsciously moved into "works." It didn't matter if my prayers and faith were answered, just as long as I "did the right thing" (a legalism system—oh, let's be honest—a religious spirit). "After all, if I am just patient, once I get to Heaven, it won't matter." Can't we see how a spirit of passivity can settle in on us? Can't we see how we can miss our inheritance here on Earth? Our faith is not rewarded. Our faith obtains.

We will live in Heaven for eternity, but we are on the earth for a short time. My mom preaches we are not humans having a spiritual experience. We are spiritual beings having a human experience.

Jesus was not striped for our healing in Heaven—there never was sickness in Heaven. He didn't become poor so that we could be rich in Heaven—there never was poverty in Heaven. Sickness and poverty are signs of the curse. Even aging is a part of the curse. Moses was 120 when he died. The Bible says his strength was not abated and his eyesight was not dimmed. Caleb, one of the two spies who wanted to take the promised land 40 years earlier, said he was as strong at 85 as he was at 40 and wanted his mountain (Joshua 14:10-12).

ABRAHAM AND SARAH

Abraham and Sarah were well past childbearing years. Sarah had ALWAYS been barren. It tells us in Romans that Abraham's body was dead, meaning he wasn't able to bring life. BUT God infused their bodies with so much life, their youth was renewed and He made Sarah's body produce when it had not in the regular process of time. She not only had a new name, but a new body. Abraham not only brought forth the promise in Isaac but had other sons with another wife after Sarah died!

WOMAN WITH THE ISSUE OF BLOOD

Imagine, the woman with the issue of blood had spent all her livelihood for 12 years to get well but was no better. She was quarantined because it was against the law to go out in public with a blood issue. She hears the stories of Jesus healing people. She hears He is coming to her town. Hope and then faith arises in her that if she can just touch the hem of His garment, she could be made well.

Think of her sitting in her house looking out the window. She might have thought, "If He wants me to be well, He will come to my house and heal me." She sees Him coming. There He is, passing right in front. She thinks, "Oh good, here He comes! Will He find me acceptable?" But wait. He's gone beyond the walk. Oh, there He goes. We can imagine the thrill as He's coming. Can she believe it? See the anticipation as He's in front. Can she even breathe? Notice the crushing disappointment as He's gone beyond the walk. Then imagine the resignation settling in after He's gone. She might have thought, "It must not be His will for me to be well. I will die in peace knowing I kept the law and I will be obedient to the will of God even unto death." Where would she have been if that was her thought process? DEAD!!!

Yet, that is not what she said. She said, "If I can touch the hem of His garment, I will be made well." She thought, "I am going to go against the law. I am going to go out there and they can stone me, but I'm going to get my healing." She took it! She got it! Not only did she get well, but Jesus said her faith had made her WHOLE. He restored her fortunes that had been spent on doctors that made her no better. There is shalom—nothing missing, nothing broken again!

Do we have trouble when we hear, "She took it?" When Jesus died, He died for the whole world. The price is paid. It's available to all, but who gets salvation? Those who take it. I am a taker of the things of God. Let me be bolder and say I'm also selfish—selfish for the things of God. I'm not waiting on someone else to get the revelations God opens; they may never get it. But if I get it, I'm taking it.

REALITY CHECK

If we were not a Christian, what about Christians would make us want to serve our God?

Do non-Christians think: "Christians seem to be as poor, sick and as clueless as everyone else. Why should I get saved just to follow a bunch of rules and things stay the same? I'm already sick, poor and clueless. I'll take my chances because there is nothing that says their God is real anyway." If people are going to reject God, let's give them something to reject.

Let's see what God will say and do in their situation. Give them a real decision to make. "Do I believe the demonstrations and take what I'm seeing and hearing and want a part of it or do I want to stay the same?" Make it an obvious choice between two roads!

- <u>Revelatory</u> – word of wisdom, word of knowledge, discerning of spirits.
- <u>Utterance</u> – tongues, interpretation of tongues, prophecy.
- <u>Power</u> – faith, gifts of healings, working of miracles.

DEMONSTRATION

The power and giftings of the Holy Spirit are for us and for our world. It is God's will that we move in this. Think of this: what if a woman gets saved and she is single and destitute, having nothing? You give her a word of wisdom to go work at a certain business. She goes and gets a job and ends up marrying the owner—a wealthy man (like the story of Ruth). Her days of loneliness and poverty are over!

Suppose a person is being tormented by a recurring dream. They say words are being spoken in a foreign tongue in the dream. They don't know what the words are, but they can tell they are not kind. You seek God and He allows you to hear the words from the dream. The interpretation is that the words are a curse. You use your authority over it, draw a bloodline around the person and cast away the spirit in the dream speaking the curses. Then you speak peace because the Lord gives His beloved sleep (Psalm 127:2) and not only their peace, but their sleep is restored.

There was a testimony from someone who worked on a prayer line of a ministry. A woman called in because she had terrible arthritis and was in constant pain. She needed healing. The counselor prayed for her, then asked her how she was. She said, "It's 10:30." He thought she must have misunderstood, but that meant she was in a different time zone. Again, he asked how she was and she repeated, "It's 10:30." After the silence on the line, she said, "You don't understand. I was blind, but now I can see the clock on the wall!" God not only healed the arthritis, but also her blindness, which wasn't even in the prayer for the arthritis. That's our generous God!

We had a visiting minister in our church and were having tremendous meetings. One of the young ladies turned to her mother during the service and said, "Mom, something's going on in my mouth." She had a split in her front teeth and her teeth had grown together—no prayer offered. The Healer was present.

My grandfather wore glasses. He was sitting in church one night while someone else was speaking. All of a sudden, his glasses fogged up and he couldn't see. He took them off, cleaned them and put them back on. He still could not see through the fog. He then realized it wasn't fog on his glasses. His eyes had been healed and what he thought was fog was blurriness because his eyes no longer needed the correction. Again, no prayer was offered.

Peter walked down the street and people were healed when his shadow fell over them!

> *"so that they brought the sick out into the streets and laid them on beds and couches, that at least the shadow of Peter passing by might fall on some of them. Also a multitude gathered from the surrounding cities to Jerusalem, bringing sick people and those who were tormented by unclean spirits, and they were all healed"* (Acts 5:15-16).

See, the power God wants to release into the lives of people, saved and unsaved?

LIFE OF CHRIST GOOD FOR ALL

The world needs the Body of Christ moving in the power of the Holy Ghost. Look at abortion. We know that over 60,000,000 babies were aborted in the U.S. alone. How many presidents or inventors or physicians and great men and women of God have been denied their expression of life on the earth? Abortion is not about people making right decisions. God made women to be mothers—nurturing and loving. Abortion is deep, dark witchcraft deceiving these women created to be loving and nurturing to voluntarily line up to have life ripped from their wombs; not only cutting off the child, but also the purpose of the woman in the earth. The woman may go on to have other children, but she will never be "Bobby's mother" (or whatever the child's name may have been) on earth. See what God did? He overturned Roe v. Wade in the U.S. from being one national law and broke it into 50 pieces by sending it back to the individual States to make judgment on it.

The world needs the Body of Christ manifesting the Holy Spirit of God and setting people free!

THIRD GREAT AWAKENING

We are poised for a third great awakening. God is moving us there, whether we are ready or not. He says there is a billion-soul harvest about to come into the Kingdom. It's "all hands on deck."

Imagine 2,000 years of the gospel of Jesus Christ and over 6,000 years of God's hand working and planting in the earth and we have yet to see the harvest. It's about to spring forth. We need the power of the Kingdom of Heaven working in us to bring in and process the harvest.

God prophetically said a few years ago He was bringing a billion-soul harvest. I'm asking God for a four-billion-soul harvest. If Abraham could bargain with God for less righteous in Sodom and Gomorrah to save the city, why can't we ask God to harvest MORE than a billion? After all, it's His will that none should perish. Then the four billion, added to those who are already saved, minister to others and even more are saved!

NO CHRISTIAN THEORY

I am not interested in living a life of Christian theory—it "should have" worked that way. I'm interested in God moving through me to liberate captives and heal the sick. Let's use our faith, authority and power. Jesus didn't send out the disciples to pray for the sick. He told them to HEAL THE SICK.

> *"Heal the sick, cleanse the lepers, raise the dead, cast out demons. Freely you have received, freely give"*
> (Matthew 10:8).

These were men Jesus was sending out who weren't filled with the Spirit. They weren't even "saved" (they were righteous under the law) because Jesus had not died yet. Let's take what the Holy Spirit has given us and manifest these giftings for ourselves and for all of creation!

> *"The entire universe is standing on tiptoe, yearning to see the unveiling of God's glorious sons and daughters!"*
> (Romans 8:19 TPT).

Section VI

To Catch a Thief

Chapter Seventeen

The Thief Must Repay

"... when he (a thief) is found, he must repay seven times [what he stole]; He must give all the property of his house [if necessary to meet his fine]"
(Proverbs 6:31 AMP) (emphasis mine).

WARNING: THIS GRAPHIC CHAPTER WILL TRIGGER A RELIGIOUS SPIRIT

Why the warning? The enemy does not want us to know who we are or what we have so he wraps many "beliefs" we hold dear in religious jargon and the traditions of men that are not scriptural and are dead. However, God wants us free. He sent Jesus to do it, so let's walk in it.

WE'VE BEEN ROBBED

We've been robbed. Whether we know it or not, we have. The biggest theft happened in the beginning—our relationship with God—and we still live with that theft if we do not receive the return of that relationship through Jesus Christ, the only begotten Son of God, our Savior and Lord!

In order to recover goods that have been stolen, we need to know what was ours to begin with so we can have a true accounting of the theft. If our grandfather had owned a Picasso painting, but we did not know it, we could walk through a warehouse of stolen goods and not claim it as ours, so therefore, it would not be returned to us and our family.

THE INVENTORY

1) Relationship with God
2) Dominion – discussed in Chapter 8
3) Relationships – it's not good that man is alone
4) Health
5) Wholeness – nothing missing/nothing nroken
6) Prosperity and Provision
7) Purpose
8) Callings
9) Destiny (Jeremiah 29:11). God has good plans for us.
10) Power through the Holy Ghost
    - Revelatory Giftings
    - Power Giftings
    - Utterance Giftings

If God wanted this for us, wouldn't He have stated it? Yes, He did it again and again and then had Jesus reiterate it.

> *"So it shall be, when the LORD your God brings you into the land of which He swore to your fathers, to Abraham, Isaac, and Jacob, to give you large and beautiful cities which you did not build, houses full of all good things, which you did not fill, hewn-out wells which you did not dig, vineyards and olive trees which you did not plant—when you have eaten and are full— then beware, lest you forget the LORD who brought you out of the land of Egypt, from the house of bondage"*
> (Deuteronomy 6:10-12).

God warns them not to forget Him WHEN (not if) they prosper!

Look in Deuteronomy 28 (this is under the Old Covenant so this is about obeying the Law, but the New Covenant contains the same blessings through believing in Jesus Christ):

"...*The LORD your God will set you high above all nations of the earth*. And all these blessings shall come upon you and overtake you, because you obey the voice of the LORD your God: Blessed shall you be in the city, and blessed shall you be in the country. Blessed shall be the fruit of your body, the produce of your ground and the increase of your herds, the increase of your cattle and the offspring of your flocks. Blessed shall be your basket and your kneading bowl. Blessed shall you be when you come in, and blessed shall you be when you go out. The Lord will cause your enemies who rise against you to be defeated before your face; they shall come out against you one way and flee before you seven ways. The LORD will command the blessing on you in your storehouses and in all to which you set your hand, and He will bless you in the land which the LORD your God is giving you. The LORD will establish you as a holy people to Himself, just as He has sworn to you, if you keep the commandments of the LORD your God and walk in His ways. Then all peoples of the earth shall see that you are called by the name of the LORD, and they shall be afraid of you. And the LORD will grant you plenty of goods, in the fruit of your body, in the increase of your livestock, and in the produce of your ground, in the land of which the LORD swore to your fathers to give you. The LORD will open to you His good treasure, the heavens, to give the rain to your land in its season, and to bless all the work of your hand. You shall lend to many nations, but you shall not borrow. And the LORD will make you the head and not the tail; you shall be above only, and not be beneath, if you heed the commandments of the LORD your God, which I command you today, and are careful to observe them"

(Deuteronomy 28:1-13) (emphasis mine).

God loves us and has good thoughts and intentions toward us. Blessings, blessings and more blessings He wants to bestow upon us.

It is the goodness of God that leads to repentance! It is the demonstration and manifestation of His goodness that draws people to Him, not His harsh judgment. Ninevah was given three days to repent (remember Sodom and Gomorrah were not). This time of grace caused them to repent and put off the judgment of God, making Jonah look like a false prophet.

MAKE THE WORLD JEALOUS

God wants our lives to reflect His goodness and draw people to Him.

> *"Now thanks be to God who always leads us in triumph in Christ, and THROUGH US diffuses the fragrance of His knowledge in every place. For we are to God the fragrance of Christ among those who are being saved and among those who are perishing"*
> (II Corinthians 2:14-15) (emphasis mine).

Wouldn't it be great to have the fragrance of Christ upon us like the fragrance of Cinnabon in the mall? We smell the cinnamon buns and we begin to salivate. The next thing we know, we are walking through the mall looking for the cinnamon buns. Imagine people being drawn to us because His fragrance, His light and His love are emanating from us!

Let's look at an incident in Genesis 26 with Isaac:

> *"There was a famine in the land, besides the first famine that was in the days of Abraham. And Isaac went to Abimelech king of the Philistines, in Gerar. Then the LORD appeared to him and said: 'Do not go down to Egypt; live in the land of*

which I shall tell you. Dwell in this land, and I will be with you and bless you; for to you and your descendants I give all these lands, and I will perform the oath which I swore to Abraham your father. And I will make your descendants multiply as the stars of heaven; I will give to your descendants all these lands; and in your seed all the nations of the earth shall be blessed; <u>because Abraham obeyed My voice and kept My charge, My commandments, My statutes, and My laws</u>" (Genesis 26:1-5) (emphasis mine).

Wait! Didn't Abraham lie about Sarah, his wife, being his sister? Didn't he try to make the promise come to pass through a concubine and brought forth Ishmael? Yet, here is God recounting to Isaac that Abraham obeyed His voice and kept His charge, commandments, statutes, and laws! Abraham had repented so this is God's testimony of Abraham. What's His testimony of you? Actions repented of are not only forgiven but washed away. His promise is not to remember them anymore.

Now, the apple doesn't fall far from the tree. Watch what Isaac does:

"So Isaac dwelt in Gerar. And the men of the place asked about his wife. And he said, 'She is my sister'; for he was afraid to say, 'She is my wife,' because he thought, 'lest the men of the place kill me for Rebekah, because she is beautiful to behold.' Now it came to pass, when he had been there a long time, that Abimelech king of the Philistines looked through a window, and saw, and there was Isaac, showing endearment to Rebekah his wife. Then Abimelech called Isaac and said, 'Quite obviously she is your wife; so how could you say, 'She is my sister'?' Isaac said to him, 'Because I said, 'Lest I die on account of her.'' And Abimelech said, 'What is this you have done to us? One of the people might soon have lain with your

wife, and you would have brought guilt on us.' So Abimelech charged all his people, saying, 'He who touches this man or his wife shall surely be put to death'" (Genesis 26:6-11).

Isaac does a repeat! It even took a heathen king who was moral regarding a wife and marriage to expose Isaac. He repented—he didn't do it anymore—and look how God responded:

> "Then Isaac <u>sowed</u> in that land, <u>and reaped</u> in the same year a <u>hundredfold</u>; and the LORD blessed him. The man <u>began to prosper</u>, and <u>continued prospering</u> until he <u>became very prosperous</u>; for he had possessions of flocks and possessions of herds and a great number of servants. So the Philistines envied him" (Genesis 26:12) (emphasis mine).

The goodness of God was so abundant on Isaac that he reaped one hundredfold. He began to prosper. He continued prospering and he became very prosperous. So much that the Philistines—who were always thieves and robbers in the scriptures—ENVIED him. Shouldn't our life with God be so blessed that people without God are jealous of us? Weren't people drawn to Jesus because of the abundance pouring out of Him? Food was multiplied. People were healed, raised from the dead and set free. Demons were bound and cast out. Of course, not everyone received it and not everyone will, but it's not because it is not available to them.

Chapter Eighteen

Prosperity

Warning! Warning! This is where the heads of most Christian go "tilt." Let's see if we can diffuse this and straighten our heads a little.

God is not afraid of prosperity and provision. Money is not the root of all evil. The Bible says it is the LOVE of money that is the root of all evil. People will lie, cheat, steal, kill, and imprison or traffic others to get it! Poor people can have a love of money also. They think having money will get them out of their situation, not God. Rich people love their money because they don't need to rely on God either. Money becomes their god.

God provided for the children of Israel in the wilderness. How so? He provided a pillar of cloud by day to protect them from the heat. He gave them a pillar of fire by night that kept them warm. He gave them manna every morning and told them how much they needed to gather—whatever they needed. Their shoes and clothes did not wear out. That sounds prosperous to me!

Didn't God limit the children of Israel by what they could gather? No. He told them they could gather what they needed for that day. So, if it was Levi's birthday and they wanted to have 100 people over for a birthday party, they needed to gather more manna for that day. The only restriction was they couldn't gather today for tomorrow (except the day before the Sabbath).

There was a widow woman who was gathering sticks to make a last meal for her and her son during the drought during Elijah's time. He showed up and told her to make him a meal first, then feed her and her son. She did and her flour and oil did not run out again for the rest of the famine. Wasn't that prosperity?

The prophets were building a school. An axe head fell in the water and sank. It was borrowed. Elisha threw a stick in the water and it floated. Wasn't that prosperity because he could return the borrowed axe instead of being indebted to the owner?

Jesus fed the 5,000 and the 4,000 by multiplying the food. Isn't that prosperity?

FROM THE GARDEN

God made the Garden lush BEFORE He created man and then He put man in the midst of it:

> "The LORD God planted a garden eastward in Eden, and there He put the man whom He had formed. And out of the ground the LORD God made every tree grow that is pleasant to the sight and good for food. The tree of life was also in the midst of the garden, and the tree of the knowledge of good and evil. Now a river went out of Eden to water the garden, and from there it parted and became four riverheads. The name of the first is Pishon; it is the one which skirts the whole land of Havilah, where <u>there is gold</u>. And <u>the gold of that land is good. Bdellium and the onyx stone are there</u>"
> (Genesis 2:8-12) (emphasis mine).

God points out there was good gold in Havilah, along with bdellium and onyx. God does not tempt with evil. If gold and onyx were a problem, He would not have pointed them out.

Read this from The Passion Translation:

"Flowing from the Land of Delight was a river to water the garden, and from there, it divided into four branches. The first river, Overflowing Increase, encircles the gold-laden land of Havilah. The gold of that land is pure, with many pearls and onyx found there. The second river, Gushing, flows through the entire land of Cush. The third river, Swift Flowing, flows east of Assyria. And the fourth is the river Fruitfulness"
(Genesis 2:10-14 TPT).

Read it like this: The River of God will bring overflowing increase, gush like a geyser, and swiftly bring God's people to success and fruitfulness. (TPT Notes)

DAYS OF HEAVEN ON EARTH

God was so generous He even promised days of Heaven on the earth:

"That your days may be multiplied, and the days of your children, in the land which the LORD sware unto your fathers to give them, as the days of heaven upon the earth"
(Deuteronomy 11:21 KJV).

Jesus even reiterated this in the Lord's prayer:

"…Our Father in heaven, Hallowed be Your name. Your kingdom come. Your will be done <u>On earth as it is in heaven</u>"
(Luke 11:2) (emphasis mine).

If God did not want us having days of HEAVEN ON THE EARTH, He wouldn't have promised it in Deuteronomy or made it a matter of prayer taught by Jesus. How many millions of people have said this prayer? Jesus was not just filling a prayer with words. He meant what He said.

For over 2,000 years, people have been praying, *"On earth as it is in heaven."* Are we about to see the answer to this prayer on the earth?

TILT-TILT-TILT: JESUS WAS NOT POOR

Jesus was not poor. He became poor—divesting Himself of His Godness—to live on Earth. In Heaven, the streets were gold. Here He was walking in dirt (dead men). The Scripture says He became "poor" that we might be "rich." I know this is talking about spiritual things, BUT poverty was part of the curse. If we read in Deuteronomy 28, after all the blessings in the first 14 verses, there is a list of curses that show poverty, sickness, destruction, and death in verses 15-68. Jesus did not walk in the curses and if we are in Christ Jesus, we are not to be walking in the effects of the curses either!

> *"Christ has redeemed us from the curse of the law, having become a curse for us (for it is written, 'Cursed is everyone who hangs on a tree'),"* (Galatians 3:13).

Consider the following:

1) <u>No Room in the Inn</u>: The reason Jesus was born in the stable was because there was no room in the inn. They would not have looked for a room if they had no provision.
2) <u>Wise Men</u>: An entourage of wise men—possibly up to 75—came looking for the new-born king. They brought gifts of gold, frankincense and myrrh. Because they thought he was an earthly king, the gifts would have been appropriate for a king. They didn't show up until Jesus was around two years of age, which is why they came to the "house" where He was,

not the stable. This also explains why Herod killed the male children two years of age and under.

3) <u>"Where are you staying?"</u>: In John 1, two disciples of John asked this of Jesus after John said, "Behold the Lamb of God." They saw where He was staying and remained with Him that day. If Jesus was homeless, would they have stayed with Him? Remember, most of them thought He was coming to be king over the Romans. A homeless person would not fit that concept. Also, they would have thought if He's homeless and poor, what does He have to say to us?

Wait, didn't Jesus say He had nowhere to lay His head? Let's come to another revelation. Could it be Jesus was talking about His headship of the Body? The Body of Christ was not formed yet, so He, the Head of all things, had no place to lay His headship!

4) <u>Treasurer</u>: Jesus had a treasurer—Judas. Judas stole from the treasury. We don't need a treasurer for $1.50. We also don't steal $1.50. If that's all there is, it's not enough to steal, and it would be missed. Thieves steal when it won't be discovered!

5) <u>Loaves and Fishes</u>: The disciples asked Jesus about buying food for the 5,000. They wouldn't have had the discussion if they didn't have the money for it. Jesus showed them it's not about money; it was about the multiplication and blessing of God!

6) <u>The Guards Drew Lots for His Robe</u>: If it was a rag, none of them would have wanted it. It was a seamless robe, which was very expensive to make and own.

Jesus showed the abundance, provision and prosperity of God was in the manifestation of His power, authority and faith—not the coin in His pocket.

Do we believe God wants us to stay in sin? No, He does not. This is why Jesus came. He made the way for us to get out of sin and become restored to the Father. Then, it is the same way with poverty or sickness or lack of purpose or lack of harvest. It is not where God wants us to stay.

DISCIPLES WERE MEN OF MEANS

> *"Then Jesus said to His disciples, 'Assuredly, I say to you that it is hard for a rich man to enter the kingdom of heaven. And again I say to you, it is easier for a camel to go through the eye of a needle than for a rich man to enter the kingdom of God.' When His disciples heard it, they were greatly astonished, saying, 'Who then can be saved?' But Jesus looked at them and said to them, 'With men this is impossible, but with God all things are possible.' Then Peter answered and said to Him, 'See, we have left all and followed You. Therefore what shall we have?'"* (Matthew 19:23-27).

If the disciples were poor, wouldn't they have said, "Yeah, those rich guys aren't getting in!" Would Peter have made the statement, "We have left all and followed You." If they were poor, they wouldn't have had anything to leave!

Also, when Jesus sent out the 70 to go out into the harvest, He told them:

> *"Carry neither money bag, knapsack, nor sandals..."*
> (Luke 10:4).

If they were poor, Jesus would not have told them not to take a money bag. They would not have had one. Was this also a way to bring the disciples up in their faith? Instead of falling back on fleshly responses to people in their dire situations like money or tangible things, Jesus said whatever they do for others is coming out of their authority, not their pocket.

Wealth is a great thing, but it is also a revealer of the heart. Jesus said, "Where your treasure is, that's where your heart is." If our treasure is tangible, it can lead us away from God. Jesus said it's hard for a rich man to enter into the Kingdom. Why? Because they rely on their own means to achieve what they want and get everything they need. Instead of leading to generosity, abundance can lead to withholding because fear sets in that abundance might go away.

Wealth is simply a tool and a means of exchange. It can be a great blessing or it can be a great curse. It cannot buy the most important thing in life—relationship with God—but it can be a way to bless those around us to show the greatness of our God.

It's not hard to imagine in these times that people lose their jobs. What if our neighbor lost his job and we could offer to pay their mortgage until they get back on their feet? Would that create an open door to talk to them about the goodness of God?

BUT DIDN'T JESUS SAY...

> *"...In the world you will have tribulation; but be of good cheer, I have overcome the world"* (John 16:33).

Yes, Jesus did say that. Didn't He also tell us to be of good cheer because He has overcome that tribulating world?

Do we think because God wants to prosper us that lack is the only tribulation? Wealthy people can spend all their wealth trying to get well—it doesn't always work. The woman with the issue of blood had spent all her living on it, but she was a smart, wealthy woman. She looked to Jesus who not only healed her, but made her WHOLE—nothing missing, nothing broken.

According to Deuteronomy 28, God says we are the head and not the tail. Understand that every tail of a devil wants to take us down from that place of authority. Didn't God say He wants us to be above and not beneath? Don't we think the destroyer wants to pull us down? Everything God wants to give us and make us does not keep us from tribulation. In fact, it puts us in the crosshairs of the weapons of our enemy and paints a huge target on our back.

Look what happened with Jesus and the disciples when they went on a trip across the lake:

> *"Now it happened, on a certain day, that He got into a boat with His disciples. And He said to them, 'Let us cross over to the other side of the lake.' And they launched out. But as they sailed He fell asleep. And a windstorm came down on the lake, and they were filling with water, and were in jeopardy. And they came to Him and awoke Him, saying, 'Master, Master, we are perishing!' Then He arose and rebuked the wind and the raging of the water. And they ceased, and there was a calm. But He said to them, 'Where is your faith?...'"*
> (Luke 8:22-25).

Jesus told the disciples His intent, *"Let us cross over to the other side of the lake."* A storm arose. This wasn't just a little summer thunderstorm. These seasoned fishermen thought they were going to die. What did Jesus do? He rose in His authority and faith and rebuked the wind and the raging water and calm came. Of course, we are going to have tribulation, but in the middle of that tribulation, we understand who we are and we use our authority to calm those seas of emotions, thoughts and situations.

David said:

> *"Many are the afflictions of the righteous, But the LORD delivers him out of them all"* (Psalm 34:19).

> "...And this is the victory that has overcome the world—our faith. Who is he who overcomes the world, but he who believes that Jesus is the Son of God?" (I John 5:4-5).

We are more than conquerors because something had to be conquered. We are overcomers because something had to be overcome. We have faith because we need to believe for things we cannot see and pull them from the unseen realm into the seen realm.

DIDN'T JESUS ALSO SAY...

> "For you have the poor with you always..." (Mark 14:7).

Yes, He did, but this is not a pronouncement of prophetic destiny of poverty on some people. This is recognition that not all will follow God and prosper. Jesus could have easily said, "For you have sinners with you always..." Does that mean I should stay a sinner? Of course not. Again, it's the recognition that even though God has prepared the way for every man and woman ever born from Adam to the last man and woman to be saved, and even though we know it's not God's will that any should perish, sadly, some will.

We can't take statements out of context and make a doctrine. Another time the poor are addressed is in the story of the woman who came and anointed the feet of Jesus with ointment that was worth a year's wages. Then she dried His feet with her hair. Some became indignant and said it should have been used for the poor (probably the thief, Judas, because he saw something he could gain profit from for himself). Don't miss this: she was performing a prophetic act because she was anointing Him for His death and burial. After Jesus died and was buried, the women came to anoint His body, but He was already resurrected. The people so piously mentioning the poor never saw the prophetic.

THEOLOGY

We all have theology, but we need to listen to the Holy Spirit, so we don't get stuck in a theology. For example, God tells us in Genesis 8:22:

> *"While the earth remains, Seedtime and harvest, Cold and heat, Winter and summer, And day and night Shall not cease."*

This was God's covenant with Noah after the flood. We understand there is seedtime (planting), then time for the seed to grow, then harvest. Yet, if we get stuck in the understanding of "time," such as it takes time for the seed to grow, then we may never expect the harvest, which should surely follow. The same with tribulation. If we do not understand that God wants to bless us, then we may think it's His will for us to stay in tribulation and never come out. Yes, we will have tribulation, but it's on the way to victory!

We are stewards. Yet, if we get stuck in a theology of stewardship, we always pass everything on and never receive anything from God because we always think the blessing is to pass on. The importance in all our theology is relationship with God. God can tell us when it's time to wait. God can tell us when we are to pass blessings on and sometimes, He tells us it is to bless us! That's what David received at Ziklag. God said, "Pursue and recover ALL."

What is part of our relationship with God? We hear what He has to say in every situation. When we think we've "got it," we more than likely will "miss it!"

Chapter Nineteen

Catching the Thief

"The thief does not come except to steal, and to kill, and to destroy. I have come that they may have life, and that they may have it more abundantly" (John 10:10).

TESTIMONY

A friend of mine was out of town and ended up in the ER for several hours after a meal at a local restaurant. She finally got the bill: $4,000 for her stay in the hospital for several hours, BUT she only had to pay $210. Praise God, she didn't have to pay $4,000. What a relief. She rejoiced that she only had to pay $210 and it certainly was a blessing that the entire amount was not due. I think we've all waited for that "other shoe" to drop when dealing with unexpected health issues, car troubles or appliance breakdowns and wondering what the final payout will be.

We give God praise for every time and everywhere He provides for us. He is THE good, faithful, merciful, generous, giving, prospering, loving, kind, and trustworthy God. He is light and there is no darkness in Him. He is transparent and there is no "catch" or deceit in Him. As Jesus said in John 10:10, He came to give life and life MORE ABUNDANTLY!

However, we have an enemy that Jesus pointed out was a thief who comes to kill, steal and destroy us and everything we love and have. He's also a liar and a deceiver. Proverbs 5:23 (TPT) talks about the wicked being led astray by their foolish ways and they are carried away as hostages: *"kidnapped captives robbed of destiny."* The ultimate goal of our enemy is to stop us from fulfilling our God-ordained destiny, calling and covenant and to stop us from manifesting God's Kingdom in the earth!

Because our enemy is a deceiver, he comes in all sorts of camouflage. I Peter 5:8 says:

> *"Be sober, be vigilant; because your adversary the devil walks about like a roaring lion, seeking whom he may devour."*

Jesus is the real lion—the Lion of the Tribe of Judah.

> *"…For Satan himself transforms himself into an angel of light"* (II Corinthians 11:14).

Who is the true light? In John 8:12, Jesus said:

> *"…I am the light of the world…"*

In John 9:5, He says:

> *"As long as I am in the world, I am the light of the world."*

In Matthew 5:14, Jesus tells us that:

> *"You are the light of the world…"*

That's us.

> *"…When the enemy comes in like a flood, The Spirit of the LORD will lift up a standard against him"* (Isaiah 59:19).

Who brought the real flood to raise a standard against the demonic? God!! Keep in mind, the translators put in punctuation through the Scriptures. Let's change the punctuation here and see if it changes revelation for us:

> "When the enemy comes in, like a flood The Spirit of the Lord will lift up a standard against him."

Moving the comma from "When the enemy comes in like a flood,..." to "When the enemy comes in, like a flood..." emphasizes that God is the One who raised up a standard against the demonic and wicked during Noah's day by bringing the flood. The enemy didn't bring the flood and when he tries to bring a flood into our life, we are built solidly on the Rock and He will raise the standard again for us!

I belittled God for many years. Sometimes, I would receive money around my birthday or Christmas or even when I received a bonus. Occasionally, something would go wrong with my car or another need would pop up. My testimony was that God gave me the money even before the need arrived. Now, I look back and see that the thief had his hand in my pocket! Obviously, I didn't think God was big enough to give me birthday money or Christmas money or increase me with a bonus AND then take care of the need in addition to that!

II Corinthians 9:7 says:

> "...God loves a cheerful giver."

How does the enemy mimic that? In my friend's "testimony," she will GLADLY pay the $210 because she didn't have to pay the $4,000. She would have cheerfully given to the thief.

Sometimes, we are so blinded by "doing the right thing" (which causes us to look at our own navels), we don't see the thief stealing from us! Psalm 34:19 says:

> "Many are the afflictions of the righteous. But the LORD delivers him out of them all."

Unfortunately, we've translated that as "into everyone's life a little rain must fall." We might get so passive about that statement and get so used to living with an umbrella that we think we're supposed to LET the enemy have access and wreak havoc in our lives. Also, keep in mind the Scripture in Psalm was before Jesus defeated the devil and before He died on the cross, but they still had covenant—which we do too! THE LORD DELIVERS US OUT OF ALL OUR AFFLICTIONS!

In light of this, let's re-examine the above "testimony." Yes, it was wonderful my friend did not have to pay $4,000 and she will gladly pay the $210 in comparison, BUT she is being robbed of the $210. Her health was also attacked. Her time was taken since she had to be at the hospital for hours and then it took her several days to recover. No gun was needed. No threat. No hostages were taken. Just a misunderstood exchange that caused her to be a victim without her even knowing it! Cunning, isn't he?

Proverbs 6:31 says:

> *"Yet when he (a thief) is found, he must restore sevenfold; He may have to give up all the substance of his house."*
> (emphasis mine)

The latter part of that verse in The Passion Translation says:

> *"...his punishment and fine will cost him greatly."*

Make him pay!

FILING CLAIMS

I bought a house, new to me, in the last few years and have wonderful neighbors all around me. It's a great place to live with kids playing ball in the street, couples strolling with their pets and friendly people everywhere. I love it!

Let me present a scenario: what if one of my neighbors stole a bike from my back patio? What if they came into my yard and brazenly took it? I even have it on security footage. It's wrong. They broke the law. Yet, **if I do not press charges**, my neighbor gets away with it. I watch as they ride my bike back and forth down the street. Suddenly, the enjoyment of my neighborhood has turned sour.

Pay attention to what I just said: **"If I do not press charges, my neighbor gets away with it."** Jesus pointed out what the enemy wants to do—steal, kill and destroy. Proverbs tells us what the law would require—repayment of sevenfold of what was stolen, even if the thief has to give all the substance of his house!

> *"... when he* (a thief) *is found, he must repay seven times [what he stole]; He must give all the property of his house [if necessary to meet his fine]"*
> (Proverbs 6:31 AMP) (emphasis mine).

Even now, our culture has embraced stealing openly and made it legal. There are some cities that have made it unlawful to file a police report for anything under $700! They have legalized stealing anything worth $699.99 and under!

In the Old Testament, we hear again and again about the Philistines. They would steal from the Israelites. They would steal their harvests and their substance. Gideon was threshing in the winepress because he was trying to save his harvest from the Philistines. Shammah stood in the middle of a field of lentils and defended it against the marauding Philistines. This is a picture of our enemy: plundering and stealing what is not his because he has nothing of his own.

In the parable of the wheat and the tares, the husbandman has sown wheat, but when it grows up, there are tares among it. Later, Jesus explains the meaning of the parable.

> *"The field is the world, the good seeds are the sons of the kingdom, but the tares are the sons of the wicked one. The enemy who sowed them is the devil, the harvest is the end of the age, and the reapers are the angels"* (Matthews 13:38-39).

Did you see that? The reapers are the angels. There are good angels and fallen angels—demons! These fallen reapers want to grab our harvest and destroy it before we can get to it.

My friend and I filed a claim for sevenfold return of $210 and time wasted that day. We included all of that in the claim. How did we do that? First of all, we came to God based on the Word. Secondly, we came in the name of Jesus. We prayed:

> "In the name of Jesus, according to Proverbs 6:31, I file a claim, Father. I have found the thief. He robbed me of $210, plus my health was attacked and my time was lost. I want sevenfold in return even if it has to bankrupt the devil. Satan, release it. Repay it. I have authority over all your power (Luke 9:1). Angels, who are sent to minister for the heirs of salvation (Hebrew 1:14) and who hearken to the voice of Your Word (Psalm 103:20) which I am standing on, go gather it and bring it in. Father, thank You that You hear me. I have what I ask for in Your name (John 14:13). Amen."

Are we allowing the enemy to rob us freely and blindly? Have we become so accustomed to bad things, irritations and interruptions that we let the thief have open access to anything we have at any time? I can confidently say, "You have been robbed!" I can also confidently say that you don't have to remember every instance. God can bring recompense for things stolen for which you were even unaware.

Put up your "No Trespassing" signs to the thief and get back EVERYTHING he's stolen. Part of our covenant is Deuteronomy 28:7 (emphasis mine):

> *"The LORD will cause your enemies who rise against you to be defeated before your face; they shall come out against you one way and flee before you SEVEN ways."*

GOD WANTS TO BLESS US

God showed us with the children of Israel that He was able to make their clothes and shoes last for 40 years. What if our "stuff" should last until we are ready to get rid of it? What if nothing broke down or clothes never wore out? What if food multiplied and we didn't have to shop as often? Could this be the way our life should work? Nothing missing, nothing broken!

My dad pastored a church in Statesville, NC when I was in the first and second grades. A singing group made up of four adults was coming to sing at the church. My mom had inquired if they would need to eat before church and they said, "No." This was in the day when people didn't go out to eat. It was common for the pastor to keep and feed evangelists and singing groups in their homes. Unfortunately, the day they were to sing, they arrived just as my mom was ready to put dinner on the table. She had made enough spaghetti for the four of us—two children under the age of seven and two adults. When they showed up and she found out they had not eaten, she went in the backyard and asked God to multiply the spaghetti. At the end of the meal, there had been enough to feed six adults and two children!!

DON'T SETTLE

Here is a truth about the Kingdom of God. It is a legal system. There is a judge. There are penalties and judgments. There are rewards. There is a defending attorney—Jesus, our advocate. There is a prosecuting attorney—Satan, the accuser of the brethren.

In the earthly judicial system, when people are suing others, the one seeking recompense may want "discovery." The process of discovery requires the defendant to reveal things the other attorney requests about their holdings. Many times, they will try to settle out of court so they don't have to reveal illegal activities or other financial holdings from which monetary payment can be made.

So how would you settle with the thief in your life? For example, you are sick. You think you have cancer. The doctor says you have cancer. The scenarios that run through your head say death is imminent. Then the doctor contacts you to say he has good news. You don't have cancer. It's a blood disorder that can be treated with lifelong drugs and therapy. Yea! WAIT! DON'T SETTLE! God wants you healed and whole. It's great that you don't have cancer, but don't settle for a blood disorder and a life sentence of drugs and therapy. The settlement you want is wholeness!

NEVER HEARD OF THIS BEFORE

This probably sounds a little crazy, catching the thief, but this spiritual warfare is real and affects our lives. Jesus said the Holy Spirit had to come because He was going to lead us into all truth. There are things God doesn't reveal until certain times. For example, in Deuteronomy when God told them they were above and not beneath, the head and not the tail, He was going to bless their storehouses, etc., this was after over 400 years of slavery. He had to remind them of what life with God was about. He was bringing them into a place they, their parents, and grandparents, and grandparents' grandparents had not been in before. We have a choice to walk in new revelation and see the results or we can passively sit by never having anything change. When God began to show me this revelation of pressing charges, I put it to work, believing it and I have seen results in my life. I began to get refunds, commissions, raises, rebates, lowered rates, and finding things on sale.

Why can't we believe for scholarships, and inheritances, and contests won, and favor to be ours? Why can't God restore lands that may have been taken illegally or court cases overturned that were ruled unjustly?

MORE INVENTORY

What has the devil stolen from us? Not only is he a thief, but because we haven't been cognizant of our "inventory," we haven't even been aware of what he has stolen. If we see that God wants to bless us abundantly and even make the wicked jealous of His generosity toward us, then we can see where our lives might be lacking and realize we've had a thief in our stuff. These are some items that might be in our inventory:

- Lost time.
- Penalties.
- Interest.
- Fees.
- Lost items that had to be replaced.
- Technology that breaks down and steals our time trying to figure out what the problem is when it worked five minutes before.

- Broken items that had to be repaired or discarded and replaced.
- Lost relationships.
- Lost opportunities.
- Stolen items.
- Abandoned dreams.
- Lost or stolen promotions.
- Lost scholarships.
- Lost or stolen inheritances.
- Lost vision.
- Stolen revelation.

We all have stories. It varies from person to person, but the common denominator is the thief among us. The thief loves to cause problems and then points to us, accusing us (he is the accuser of the brethren), and then we work harder to try and make up because we think it is our fault. Round and round we go. Let's stop this merry-go-round and catch him!

PRESSING CHARGES

This is not a "one and done" kind of activity. Now that you've taken inventory and know what you should have, you can press charges. You can also keep an active inventory to go after the thief the minute he tries to steal again.

It's simple. You can pray this simple prayer or you can tailor it to your situation:

> "Father, thank You that You love me and have given me all things that pertain to life and godliness (2 Peter 1:3). I believe it is Your desire for me to be blessed and I believe that I can have days of Heaven on the earth. I have been robbed and I want to press charges.

Your Word says that when a thief is found he must repay sevenfold even to the bankruptcy of his own house. I have found the thief. I am asking for repayment and restoration of everything—KNOWN OR UNKNOWN—to be returned to me WITH INTEREST! I will not settle for anything less. In fact, plunder his kingdom and make it bankrupt! Reveal to me if I have left any openings for the thief to have easy access. I know Jesus came for me to have abundant life that is full and overflowing and I receive it. In the wonderful, powerful name of Jesus, Amen!"

Now in expectation, write the things you are expecting to be returned WITH INTEREST! God may bring other things to your mind. Note when they are returned. Date it all. And remember, you prayed and asked God for repayment and restoration of everything KNOWN or UNKNOWN. God may just have a few surprises in store for you!

_____

_____

_____

_____

_____

_____

_____

_____

_____

Section VII

Weapons of Warfare

Chapter Twenty

Kingdom

It may be surprising that the last section of this book called "Warrior School" is where we discuss our spiritual weapons. It is important for us to know who we are, what is God's plan, what is our authority, to be set free, and to have recovery and restoration for us to be the warriors the Kingdom needs.

Let me contrast the two kingdoms. Picture the most beautiful, natural scenery you can imagine. Is it a thick jungle with lush, green trees and colorful birds? Or is it majestic mountains with awe-inspiring snow-capped peaks? Or a beach with the sound of seagulls combined with the smell of the salty ocean breeze and relaxing cadence of the waves hitting the shore? Maybe it's a garden full of every imaginable flower. Could it be fields of grain blowing in the breeze ready for harvest? Possibly an African savannah teeming with wildlife? A coral reef with neon fish? The beautiful redwood forest of California? Maybe a beautiful sky at sunrise or sunset with pinks and purples! How about a herd of beautiful horses running with their hooves pounding the turf and their manes flowing behind them? Add redeemed people to these scenes. People full of life and joy. They walk in wholeness, creativity and fulfillment.

Now think of the landscape of the barren moon, not fit for anything living.

This is the stark difference between the two kingdoms. The beautiful, light, abundant, full of life landscapes are what

God imagined and created. The people are the redeemed ones that His Son came to save and return to fellowship with the Father. The enemy is not a creator. He can only try to take what is not his. Whatever he takes, he will destroy and make it like the moon because he has no truth, life or light. The moon does not even have its own light, but only reflects it.

DAVID'S ARMY

In I Samuel 22, we have the story of the beginning of David's army. David is fleeing from Saul. Saul cannot find David, but the men God wanted to be with David found him and came to him. Who were these great men?

> *"David therefore departed from there and escaped to the cave of Adullam. So when his brothers and all his father's house heard it, they went down there to him. And everyone who was in distress, everyone who was in debt, and everyone who was discontented gathered to him. So he became captain over them. And there were about four hundred men with him"*
> (I Samuel 22:1-2).

Wow! Look at the great beginning. Four hundred men came to David. Look who they were: EVERYONE who was in distress, EVERYONE who was in debt and EVERYONE who was discontented gathered to him. Great! A bunch of distressed, indebted malcontents, but through the time with David, these men became men of renown.

These are the names of the mighty men whom David had:

- ➤ Josheb-Basshebeth the Tachmonite, chief among the captains: He had killed eight hundred men at one time.
- ➤ Eleazar the son of Dodo: He arose and attacked the Philistines until his hand was weary and his hand stuck to the sword. The Lord brought about a great victory

that day; and the people returned after him only to plunder.
- Shammah the son of Agee the Hararite: He stationed himself in the middle of a field of lentils, defended it, and killed the Philistines. So, the Lord brought about a great victory.
- Three of the thirty chief men broke through the camp of the Philistines, drew water from the well of Bethlehem that was by the gate, and took it and brought it to David.
- Abishai the brother of Joab: He lifted his spear against three hundred men and killed them and won a name.
- Benaiah was the son of Jehoiada: He had killed two lion-like heroes of Moab. He also had gone down and killed a lion in the midst of a pit on a snowy day. And He killed an Egyptian, a spectacular man. The Egyptian had a spear in his hand, so he went down to him with a staff, wrested the spear out of the Egyptians hand, and killed him with his own spear.

It doesn't matter how we start out; we can become a mighty warrior by being strengthened, emboldened and victorious!

AS A LION

We learned in the last section that our enemy is a thief. He is not only a thief, but he goes about as a roaring lion. But he's not a roaring lion. The true roaring lion is the Lion of the Tribe of Judah, Jesus Christ our Lord.

> *"Be sober, be vigilant; because your adversary the devil walks about like a roaring lion, seeking whom he may devour"*
> (I Peter 5:8).

Just as a thief is an opportunist, so is this "as a" lion. He's looking to see whom he may devour. WE ARE NOT DEVIL'S FOOD! He may not devour us and ours and all that we have, but that doesn't mean he won't try.

If we think we can stay neutral, it is not possible. We are either in one kingdom or another—the mighty Kingdom of God or the lesser kingdom of Satan. We are under law or grace. Under law, we have to pay the penalty for our sin. Living under grace is when we receive the price Jesus paid for our sins. Let's choose to live under grace!

When we were born, we were born in a battle zone behind enemy lines and we were the enemy of God. Just look at God—not afraid of the enemy having a beginning advantage! But when we answer the call of the great King, His great power releases us from the lesser power of the kingdom of darkness, and He translates us into the Kingdom of His dear Son!

> *"He has delivered us from the power of darkness and conveyed us into the kingdom of the Son of His love, in whom we have redemption through His blood, the forgiveness of sins"*
> (Colossians 1:13-14).

The devil doesn't care if we get saved. If he can keep us sin conscious and looking at our own navel, we will not be occupying territory for ourselves or others nor using our authority against his rebellious tyranny. He will roam free to do as he pleases. As discussed in Section IV, Liberation, God has loosed us, so we want to free others as well! If we are only obsessed with ourselves and are in bondage to legalism of doing the "right" thing, we cannot see the bondage of others to release them to walk in the freedom of the Kingdom of God!

Chapter Twenty-One

Armor of God

God doesn't expect us to fight this spiritual war against the "as a" lion and thief with our own weapons. He has given us His armor!

If we are clothed in the whole armor of God—proper shoes, helmet, shield in front of us, and sword in our hand—who does the devil see? Does he see us or does he see God because we are in God's armor?

> *"Finally, my brethren, be strong in the Lord and in the power of His might. Put on the <u>whole armor of God</u>, that you may be able to stand against the wiles of the devil. For we do not wrestle against flesh and blood, but against principalities, against powers, against the rulers of the darkness of this age, against spiritual hosts of wickedness in the heavenly places. Therefore take up the <u>whole armor of God</u>, that you may be able to withstand in the evil day, and having done all, to stand. Stand therefore, having girded your waist with truth, having put on the breastplate of righteousness, and having shod your feet with the preparation of the gospel of peace; above all, taking the shield of faith with which you will be able to quench all the fiery darts of the wicked one. And take the helmet of salvation, and the sword of the Spirit, which is the word of God; praying always with all prayer and supplication in the Spirit…"* (Ephesians 6:10-18) (emphasis mine).

We are not talking about a walk in the park here. This passage tells us that we need not just the armor of God, but the WHOLE armor of God that we may be able to stand against the wiles of the deceptive devil. This isn't a fight against flesh, even though he tries to draw us there, but against principalities, rulers of the darkness of this age and spiritual hosts of wickedness in heavenly places.

> *"For although we live in the natural realm, we don't wage a military campaign employing human weapons, using manipulation to achieve our aims. Instead, our spiritual weapons are energized with divine power to effectively dismantle the defenses behind which people hide. We can demolish every deceptive fantasy that opposes God and break through every arrogant attitude that is raised up in defiance of the true knowledge of God. We capture, like prisoners of war, every thought and insist that it bow in obedience to the Anointed One"* (II Corinthians 10:3-5 TPT).

Our weapons are mighty in God. We cast down arguments that exalt themselves against the knowledge of God and bring those thoughts into captivity. What is this? Have you ever thought, "This will never change," "I will always be sick," "I will always be poor," "I will always be alone," "My marriage will always be miserable?" These are only a few of the thoughts that exalt themselves! What does that mean? These thoughts have absolutely NO basis in God! These thoughts are exalting themselves against and above our knowledge that God is good, He provides, He is loving, kind, healing, and miraculous. He never changes, but He does change our situations, times and seasons.

In Isaiah 54, we can see again where God has given us the victory:

> *"No weapon formed against you shall prosper, And every tongue which rises against you in judgment You shall condemn.*

This is the heritage of the servants of the LORD..."
(Isaiah 54:17).

God doesn't say there won't be weapons formed against us, but He does say they won't prosper! He always gives us the upper hand!

BREAK DOWN

Let's break down the pieces of God's armor. We are to be strong IN THE LORD and the power of HIS might. It's not our will and our physical strength that wins. If that is the case, then anyone with a strong will and emotional strength can defeat the enemy. Not true!

We want the whole armor of God, not just bits or pieces. Having this, we can stand!

Stand: Have we ever seen an army lying down? Even if a soldier is in a prone position, such as a sniper or scout position, he is alert and ready for war. Standing is a formidable weapon. A group of soldiers standing are not easily overtaken. Just their position shows they are not at rest or unaware of their surroundings.

Gird your waist with truth: This was a belt that all the other pieces of armor hinged on. The belt covered the area where the productive organs are. We must hold ourselves together and put all our other pieces of armor on the truth of Jesus Christ and His Word! As we add revealed truths, we add to that which girds us up. Then this truth, which will come out of our mouth, causes us to hear the word of faith, which causes more faith to come, causing more truth to be established in us!

"For precept must be upon precept, precept upon precept, Line upon line, line upon line, Here a little, there a little"
(Isaiah 28:10).

Put on the breastplate of righteousness: The accuser of the brethren comes to accuse us and remind us of our failures and past faults. It is not the breastplate of our righteousness, but the breastplate of His righteousness. When the enemy accuses us to discourage us and make us think we've "missed it," we have to know it's His righteousness and Jesus never "missed it!"

Shod your feet with the preparation of the gospel of peace: Everywhere our feet go, we walk in love and leave peace behind. In Matthew 5:9, Jesus said, *"Blessed are the peacemakers..."* Unfortunately, we've become peacekeepers. There is a difference between peacemakers and peacekeepers. There are times we must go to war to make peace. Look at history. An enemy arises, which causes those who don't want to go to war to have to take up arms. If we don't protect our peace, our land, our way of life by going to war, our enemy will take over and force his idea of living upon us. Even though our way of life as a Christian is peace, it is not peace at any cost and we war against the enemies of God. Peace at any cost means we will surrender our position to keep peace. This is not an acceptable option.

Take the shield of faith to quench all the fiery darts of the wicked one: Think of flaming arrows that the enemy launches at us. One after another after another. Our shield of faith, believing God and what He has said and His love for us, quenches and disables the arrows and keeps them from hitting their mark. But even if they do get through, God is the Healer!!

> *"Beloved, do not think it strange concerning the fiery trial which is to try you, as though some strange thing happened to you;"* (I Peter 4:12).

Peter tells us it's not strange to have fiery trials. Even during great trials, God is so great that He promises us in Romans 8:28:

> "...we know that all things work together for good to those who love God, to those who are the called according to His purpose."

That's us. We love God and we are called according to His purpose, so we know He's working all things for our good.

The Scripture in I Peter 4 means a lot to my family. God gave that Scripture to my dad to preach when my grandmother had been given three days to live. She was filled with cancer. "Somehow" within those three days, the cancer "disappeared" and my grandmother lived whole over 30 more years! It was truly a miracle, which was written in her file at St. Joseph's Hospital in Tampa, Florida. I Peter 4:12 was just the Word we needed to strengthen our shields of faith.

Take the helmet of salvation: Salvation is more than going to heaven. It is protection and provision and healing. It comes from the Greek word "soteria" meaning safety, health and deliverance. We keep that helmet on our heads and around our minds not letting in the thoughts of discouragement and defeat. We must pay attention to our thoughts. What are our thoughts saying? Sometimes, we have thoughts playing in the backgrounds of our mind of which we are not even aware. Possibly, we were told by a parent or someone we trusted, "you will never amount to anything" or "you are a bad person." If we have not dispelled these lies, they can play as "white noise" in the background of our thinking. We meditate on those thoughts without even realizing it. Because it might have been a parent or someone we thought highly of, we received their criticism as truth. Along with fear, this is a way the enemy "softens" the ground for his attacks.

Here is a tricky way the enemy comes at us. He interjects a thought. The devil can't read our mind. He suggests things and our actions can tell him whether we have accepted his suggestion. For example, if he introduces a fear that we have cancer, when we run to the phone and make a doctor's appointment, he knows his fearful suggestion has hit its mark.

When a thought comes in, then an emotion attaches to it. A thought and an emotion are hard to overcome. For example, if we hear (again), we will never amount to anything and an emotion of discouragement or failure accompanies it, we might just give in to these lies—both thoughts and emotions. Discouragement is a temptation. The thought comes. The enemy shows why we should be discouraged and we either yield to the temptation or we can be like David who encouraged himself in the Lord. Please do not think this is a light thing. However, we must stand against our enemy if we ever want to see him defeated. He will not leave on his own and the Lord can give us strategies to set ambushes against him!

In II Kings 6, a band of Syrian raiders had been coming against Israel. The king of Syria would tell his servants where he would make camp. Every time, the Lord would tell Elisha where this army camped. Elisha would then tell the king of Israel so his army would not get caught in an ambush. The king of Syria thought someone was divulging his secrets, but he was told the birds carried the plans discussed in his bedchamber to Elisha, the prophet. The king of Syria sent an army to capture Elisha. Here's what happened:

> *"Therefore he sent horses and chariots and a great army there, and they came by night and surrounded the city. And when the servant of the man of God arose early and went out, there was an army, surrounding the city with horses and chariots. And his servant said to him, 'Alas, my master! What shall we do?'*

So he answered, 'Do not fear, for those who are with us are more than those who are with them.' And Elisha prayed, and said, 'LORD, I pray, open his eyes that he may see.' Then the LORD opened the eyes of the young man, and he saw. And behold, the mountain was full of horses and chariots of fire all around Elisha. So when the Syrians came down to him, Elisha prayed to the LORD, and said, 'Strike this people, I pray, with blindness.' And He struck them with blindness according to the word of Elisha. Now Elisha said to them, 'This is not the way, nor is this the city. Follow me, and I will bring you to the man whom you seek.' But he led them to Samaria. So it was, when they had come to Samaria, that Elisha said, 'LORD, open the eyes of these men, that they may see.' And the LORD opened their eyes, and they saw; and there they were, inside Samaria! Now when the king of Israel saw them, he said to Elisha, 'My father, shall I kill them? Shall I kill them?' But he answered, 'You shall not kill them. Would you kill those whom you have taken captive with your sword and your bow? Set food and water before them, that they may eat and drink and go to their master.' Then he prepared a great feast for them; and after they ate and drank, he sent them away and they went to their master. So the bands of Syrian raiders came no more into the land of Israel"
(II Kings 6:14-23).

See how fear came into the servant of Elisha because of what he saw? But Elisha saw more. He asked God to let the servant see that there were more for them than against them. A plan was to take the enemy right into the heart of Israel. They fed them and gave them water, then let them go and the raiders never came again. God can let us see there are more for us, blind our enemy and give us a strategy to oust him!

If we are not established in truth about what God says about us, then the lies from our enemy can be wreaking havoc in our lives. We ask the Holy Spirit to expose the lies. Instead of our minds talking to us, we talk to our minds. We don't let random thoughts come in. We tell our minds what to think. We rehearse truth, which can be the identity markers we learned about in Chapter 4, Identity Markers, and/or particular words the Lord gives us.

HALT! WHO GOES THERE? STATE YOUR BUSINESS!

We cannot allow our thoughts to be on "cruise" and just go wherever they want. We must consider ourselves on sentry duty. If we were just average people with no training, we might miss the signs of a suspicious thought. However, because we are training to be warriors for the Kingdom of God, we need to examine every thought that comes across our mind. Even though a new sentry might find this overwhelming, the trained eye knows the things that are important and the things that can be dismissed. Additionally, we have the Holy Spirit that leads us into all truth. He can highlight those thoughts that are toxic and have potentially neutralizing or even deadly effects.

We have "white noise" thoughts which can be discouraging thoughts. Discouraging thoughts come to everyone. It's what we do with those thoughts that make the difference. Toxic "white noise" is us hearing "you can't," "things won't ever change," "this is your life, accept it." After a while, when those discouraging, defeating thoughts have accomplished their purpose, we don't even attempt to change or rise above the discouragement and move into acceptance.

The next time a discouraging thought comes, BLOCK IT. Say HALT! Make it declare who it is: WHO GOES THERE? Make it state its intent: WHAT IS YOUR BUSINESS? If it does not line up with the Word of God and if it is not something God would lovingly say to you, deny the thought access and replace the thought with a truth from God—an identity marker!!!! You will be surprised at how many discouraging or even prideful thoughts take up brain and emotional space!!

The devil thinks he can live rent free in our mind and emotions! Not so. It may be rent free for our enemy, but it costs us everything—destiny, prosperity, health, fulfillment, etc.

SWORD OF THE SPIRIT

The sword of the Spirit, which is the Word of God, is listed in Ephesians 6:17 (TPT):

> *"...And take the mighty razor-sharp Spirit-sword of the spoken word of God."*

What do we do when we are under attack? Do we go into a defensive posture, like an animal on his back? Do we begin to pray and ask God to intervene on our behalf? Or do we use our weapons?

The enemy puffs himself up to make himself look huge and it would be easy to throw down our weapons and run. Remember, spirits never come alone. The demonic sends out the spirit of fear first. This spirit wants to paralyze us and terrorize us so much we can't think straight to pick up our weapons. Then the discourager opens his mouth:

"God won't do this for you."
"Remember so and so and what happened to them?"
"This is a bunch of silly gobblety goop."
"This is too much for you to handle."

See, he's sending an attack to soften the ground to make it easy for the enemy just to march right in and take from us without any resistance. Ephesians 6:17 tells us not only is the Word of God mighty, it's razor sharp AND IT'S SPOKEN! A Bible sitting on our nightstand never mixed with faith does us no good!!!

AUTHORITY - USE IT

Paul tells us in I Thessalonians 5:17 to pray without ceasing, BUT there are times we pray and there are times we speak. Jesus told us in Mark 11:

> *"...Have faith in God. For assuredly, I say to you, whoever says to this mountain, 'Be removed and be cast into the sea,' and does not doubt in his heart, but believes that those things he says will be done, he will have whatever he says. Therefore, I say to you, whatever things you ask when you pray, believe that you receive them, and you will have them"* (Mark 11:22-24).

Notice, Jesus didn't say, "**Whoever PRAYS to God about the mountain**, he will have whatever he prays." He said, "**Whoever SAYS to this mountain**, 'Be removed and be cast into the sea,' and does not doubt in his heart, but believes that those things he says will be done, **he will have whatever he SAYS**!" What are we saying?

THE RED SEA

The children of Israel were facing the Egyptians as the Egyptians closed them in with their backs to the Red Sea and they were terribly afraid (again, fear):

> *"And when Pharaoh drew near, the children of Israel lifted their eyes, and behold, the Egyptians marched after them. So*

they were very afraid, and the children of Israel cried out to the LORD. Then they said to Moses, 'Because there were no graves in Egypt, have you taken us away to die in the wilderness? Why have you so dealt with us, to bring us up out of Egypt? Is this not the word that we told you in Egypt, saying, 'Let us alone that we may serve the Egyptians'? For it would have been better for us to serve the Egyptians than that we should die in the wilderness"* (Exodus 14:10-12).

They were facing a spiritual enemy clothed in flesh! Listen to Moses:

"And Moses said to the people, 'Do not be afraid. Stand still, and see the salvation of the LORD, which He will accomplish for you today. For the Egyptians whom you see today, you shall see again no more forever. The LORD will fight for you, and you shall hold your peace" (Exodus 14:13-14).

Whew hoo! Go, Moses! Wasn't that a rousing speech about what God was going to do? Yeah! Go, God!!

What did God say to Moses? Read on:

"And the LORD said to Moses, 'Why do you cry to Me? Tell the children of Israel to go forward. But lift up your rod, and stretch out your hand over the sea and divide it. And the children of Israel shall go on dry ground through the midst of the sea" (Exodus 14:15-16).

Moses was encouraging the children of Israel to see what God was going to do (be a spectator) and then God chides Moses to hold up his rod, stretch out his hand and to divide the Red Sea! God is looking for our involvement and cooperation. He instructed Moses to be active in this battle.

"'…The word is near you, in your mouth and in your heart' (that is, the word of faith which we preach):"
(Romans 10:8).

The Word, this mighty, razor sharp Spirit-sword, is in our own mouth.

MAKE SOME NOISE

A sword being pulled from a scabbard makes a noise. The metal on metal being scraped as the blade is unsheathed can be heard. It can be a terrifying sound, especially if we are unarmed or unskilled. What kind of sound are we making when we are under attack? Do we let the devil know the blade is coming? Let him hear us unsheathing our weapon. Let him know we are not easy prey.

How many Christians know the Word? If Ephesians tells us that the sword of the Spirit is the Word of God and we don't know the Word of God, how do we stand? The sword is not just the Word of God in written form. Not much damage can be done with the book in hand. The sword Paul is talking about here is an audible, verbal Word of God.

We can war with the Word of God, whether written in the Bible or a Word God has spoken and revealed to us. Hear that Word. Rehearse that Word. Meditate on that Word. It becomes another "jab" of the sword we can use.

A DREAM

A couple of years ago, I was going through a discouraging time. Things were not happening as I had hoped or thought. I was not suicidal, but I told God if this was all there was, why didn't He just take me on to Heaven? The Word says with long life He would satisfy me, but I wasn't satisfied. I then had a dream. In my dream, I purchased something and from the change I figured out how much I paid—$26.19. When I woke up, I remembered I had read where people said God spoke numbers in their dreams and they would look them up in Scripture and it would be a Word for them. I decided to check it out. Isaiah is always a good place to start, so I went there first. This is the first line of Isaiah 26:19: *"Your dead shall live."* I about jumped out of bed! Here I was concerned about things being dead and finished, and God said my dead shall live.

That is now a sword for me. When the enemy comes at me and tries to discourage me with "see this" and "see that," I have a personal Word (sword) that I wield. I not only wield that sword, but I also use that Word to speak words of resurrection like Jesus with Lazarus: finances, come forth; relationships, live; destiny and callings, come forth and live!!!

USE THE SWORD

When I was pregnant with my middle daughter, Jessica, God impressed Romans 8:2 to my heart:

> *"For the law of the Spirit of life in Christ Jesus has made me free from the law of sin and death."*

I began to rehearse that Scripture over and over. Notice again how the Kingdom of God is above and releases us from the lesser kingdom. I rehearsed this for about three months. I have to say that fear tried to get a foothold because God was talking about death here—not something anyone wants to hear, but especially a pregnant woman! But, I believed God had good in store for me, which was why He gave me a Word about the LAW of the Spirit of LIFE.

After Jessica was born, they had a team of nurses working on her for some issues, which turned out to be nothing, but I was still speaking that Scripture! After they moved me from the birthing room to my private room, I didn't feel like I was getting enough oxygen when I was breathing. I didn't hyperventilate. I just wasn't getting a full breath of satisfying oxygen. I was still meditating on Romans 8:2—whatever was going on, the LAW of the Spirit of life in Christ Jesus had set me free from the LAW of sin and death.

A nurse came into my room and never left. Then they moved me to the heart unit on a different floor. I had to call my husband and parents to tell them I was in another room. They put a monitor on my finger to measure the amount of oxygen in my blood, which beeped all night long, keeping me awake. A pulmonary doctor came in and checked me out. The next morning, the OB doctor came in to tell me I had given them a scare. Apparently, when I was pushing for Jessica's birth, some of the amniotic fluid had seeped into my bloodstream. Most of the time when this happens, the amniotic fluid settles on the mother's lungs and she smothers. Nurses will find a new mother dead because it's a silent killer.

We had friends who were missionary doctors and when my mom shared the story, they said we had a miracle! I believe God had given me that sword of the Word of Romans 8:2 to continually say over myself and gave me a miracle before I ever knew I was going to need it! The enemy was trying to take me and my daughter out! The sword (Word) was victorious!

I was pregnant again several years later. The doctor had said that the amniotic embolism incident was an isolated condition and even though someone had it once, it wasn't an automatic problem for the next childbirth. When I was ready to push with my third daughter, the amniotic sac distended out of my body and the amniotic fluid drained. There was no amniotic fluid to get into my bloodstream with this childbirth. That Scripture worked for the birth of my second daughter and then for my third daughter, four years later!

JESUS USED HIS SWORD

When Jesus was driven into the wilderness to be tempted by the devil, what did He do? He spoke the Word of God. "It is written…," "It is written again…," and finally, "Away with you, Satan! For it is written…" He was in warfare with Satan, just like we are in warfare with Satan. This is how people of God defeat the enemy. They use their swords! Notice, Jesus didn't kill the devil because the devil is an eternal being that will be dealt with at the end of time. The use of the sword of the Spirit caused the devil to leave until a more opportune time. We don't kill the devil or demons because they are eternal beings. We occupy territory or they occupy territory!

PREPARED SWORDS

Several years ago, I was the associate pastor and worship leader at our church. The Lord impressed me to have the congregation say scriptures one hundred times a day. Each Sunday, I would have a verse or verses for us to rehearse one hundred times a day each week. It would take about ten minutes through the course of the day. I would say it a few times while getting ready in the morning. Then I would say it in the car on the way to work and on the way home from work. Then again on the way to lunch, etc. A little over a year later, I knew the time for this was over. Anyone participating had said Scripture over 100,000 times!! What were we doing? We were sharpening our swords. We were practicing with our swords so they were at the ready.

Soldiers learn their weapons. They clean them. They take them apart and put them back together in the dark. They target shoot. They know them inside and out. Why? So, when they are in battle, they not only access their weapons readily, but they can load them and fix them if there are issues.

This is one of the things we are learning with the identity markers. We are not only learning who we are but sharpening our sword so when the enemy comes to lie to us, we can come against him with who God says we are!

LIVING AND POWERFUL

Our sword of the Spirit is not just words on a page or positive thinking.

> *"For the word of God is living and powerful, and sharper than any two-edged sword, piercing even to the division of soul and spirit, and of joints and marrow, and is a discerner of the thoughts and intents of the heart"* (Hebrews 4:12).

> *"'Is not My word like a fire?' says the LORD, 'And like a hammer that breaks the rock in pieces?'"* (Jeremiah 23:29).

The Word is alive! It pierces and divides soul and spirit. Remember, a bad thought will connect with an emotion. Our soul is our mind, will and emotions. The Word can separate them and instead of our emotions ruling over us, the sword of the Spirit sets us free to be the head and not the tail!

WORDS ARE IMPORTANT

Are our words important? Oh yes, they are. God only says those things He expects to come to pass! When God saw the earth, He didn't say, "Oh wow, look how dark it is!" He said, "Let there be light," and light came. He said what He wanted! Again, we must listen to our words. What are we saying?

Are we saying, "I'm old?" The Word says:

> *"Who* (God) *satisfies your mouth with good things, So that your youth is renewed like the eagle's"*
> (Psalm 103:5) (emphasis mine).

Notice our mouth is satisfied with good things so we will talk about good things, so our youth is renewed.

Are we saying, "I'm learning this too late. Too many years have passed." The Word says:

"So I will restore to you the years that the swarming locust has eaten, The crawling locust, The consuming locust, And the chewing locust..." (Joel 2:25).

"They shall still bear fruit in old age; They shall be fresh and flourishing," (Psalm 92:14).

Are we saying, "I'm afraid." The Word says:

"For God has not given us a spirit of fear, but of power and of love and of a sound mind" (II Timothy 1:7).

Are we saying, "I don't know what to do." The Word says:

"If any of you lacks wisdom, let him ask of God, who gives to all liberally and without reproach, and it will be given to him" (James 1:5).

Are we saying, "I don't have anything." The Word says:

"And my God shall supply all your need according to His riches (not according to my needs) *in glory by Christ Jesus"* (Philippians 4:19) (emphasis mine).

These are a few Scriptures we can add to our swords and cast down those thoughts that exalt themselves above the knowledge of God!

Don't forget this sword:

"...what seems impossible to you is never impossible to God!" (Matthew 19:26 TPT).

WHAT WEAPONS? WHAT STRONGHOLDS?

"For the weapons of our warfare are not carnal but mighty in God for pulling down strongholds," (II Corinthians 10:4).

This Scripture tells us there are weapons of warfare for pulling down strongholds. This begs us to ask the question: what weapons and what strongholds? There is no set answer for this.

Yes, we have our shield of faith and our sword of the Spirit, but what is God wanting us to particularly use in our situation? As we saw in the story of II Kings with Elisha, God has strategies to disarm our enemies and turn them away.

Our walk with the Lord is just that, a walk with the Lord. It's not the "I've got it, I can take it from here" walk, but we walk in communion with our Lord and Savior. Yes, we always need to live in faith, but what does God say today for us to use in our shield of faith and our sword of the Spirit? Just like God gave the children of Israel manna every day, God wants to commune with us every day. He wants us to have what we need for today with the confidence, assurance and faith that what we need for tomorrow will be there as well.

Keep a notebook to write down what God says. Don't forget to date it. It's amazing how much can be stolen from us. Go back and read your notes. You will probably find dreams or words you had totally forgotten about. Writing down what God says to you is also a way of showing Him that what He says is important enough for you to want to remember. The thief certainly wants to steal anything God says to you. Write it down because, after all, it is God speaking to you!

We only read of one Red Sea, one Jericho, one Daniel in the den of lions, one Gideon, one sound in the mulberry trees because God has millions of ways to work in our situations. He wants to show Himself glorious and victorious in us, with us and on our behalf.

We come to the end of our training. God has provided all the things necessary for our victory. I John 3:8 says:

"...For this purpose the Son of God was manifested, that He might destroy the works of the devil" (I John 3:8).

Our foe is already defeated. We are warriors to occupy until Jesus returns!

Warriors, arise!

MY SWORD (List Scriptures here that are the sword you wield by faith)

About the Author

Rev. Dr. Debbie Brewer has been an associate pastor, a worship leader and is a Bible teacher. She leads a group called, The Hub, equipping saints for spiritual life in the 21st Century. She is passionate about her faith and her favorite saying is, "I'm coming after You, God!" She loves to teach and see people's lives changed as they receive revelation and have transformation.

Debbie can be contacted at www.clifeministries.com or via email at revdeb@clifeministries.org.